VALOUR
ON
JUNO BEACH

THE CANADIAN AWARDS FOR GALLANTRY

D-DAY
JUNE 6, 1944

T. Robert Fowler

Published by

GENERAL STORE
PUBLISHING HOUSE

499 O'Brien Rd., Box 415, Renfrew, Ontario, Canada K7V 4A6
Telephone (613) 432-7697 or 1-800-465-6072
www.gsph.com

ISBN 1-896182-02-X
Printing by Custom Printers of Renfrew Ltd.

Layout and Design by Mervin Price
Cover Design by Leanne Enright

Copyright © 1994
The General Store Publishing House
Renfrew, Ontario, Canada

Canadian Cataloguing in Publication Data

Fowler, T. Robert
    Valour on Juno Beach: D-Day, June 6, 1944

Includes index.
ISBN 1-896182-02-X

Cover Photo Credit: THE CANADIAN MEMORIAL CROSS
Copyright THE CANADIAN WAR MUSEUM/ Photography by William Kent

    1. World War, 1939-1945—Campaigne—France—Normandy.
2. Canada. Canadian Army—History—World War, 1939-1945.
3. World War, 1939-1945—Medals. I. Title

D756.5.N6F69 1994   940.54'2144'2   C94-900382-4

First Printing May 1994
Second Printing January 2005

Also by the author:

VALOUR IN THE
VICTORY CAMPAIGN:
Gallantry Decorations of the 3rd
Canadian Infantry Division in 1945

Table of Contents

CHAPTER   *PAGE*

1   The Canadian Forces   1
2   OVERLORD - The Invasion of France   5
3   The 6th of June - Assault from the Sky
         Airborne Assault   11
         The Tactical Air Support   16

4   The 6th of June - Assault from the Sea   19
         Red Beach of Nan Sector   25
         White Beach of Nan Sector   36
         Green Beach of Nan Sector   43
         Red and Green Beaches of Mike Sector   47
         The Western Flank of Mike Sector   56

5   The 6th of June - The Advance Inland
         Moving Out of Bernières   59
         Assault on the Tailleville Position   61
         The Advance to Colomby-sur-Thaon/Anguerny   66
         Advance on the Right Flank   67
         The Beachhead Consolidated   68

6   Commanders Receiving Awards   73
7   Extraordinary Awards   81
8   The Final Action   83
9   The End of D-Day   87

Abbreviations   89
Index of Awards   91
Index of Formations   95
Appendix - The Awards   97
Bibliography   103

Foreword

VALOUR ON JUNO BEACH

To read this book is probably the closest a person could come to living — or reliving — the experience of the Canadians who landed in Normandy in June of 1944.

The author, perhaps unknowingly, starts to capture the flavour of the invasion when he mentions the "Prussian grey" shoulder flashes, and the respect shown to the men of the 3rd Canadian Infantry Division who wore them, as they waited in England for the "it's on" signal.

The 3rd Division, and the other formations taking part — such as the First Paras and J-Force of the Navy — were a close knit family with a strong esprit de corps developed during the many months of assault training in the United Kingdom. The ground troops even wore a distinctive "mercury-type" helmet!

The author has captured the essence of what these men were all about in an unique manner; and as a bonus he accurately and briefly describes the events leading up to the landing and gives the reader sufficient historical background to understand the story line.

The story is told primarily in the citations for bravery. More to the point, these stories of gallantry manage to cobble together the entire fabric of those few momentous days in our history.

To read of these deeds is to understand this tragic but magnificent episode— from the landing of the paratroops, to the task of the landing ships manned by the Navy, to the bombardment by the gunners, to the destruction of the beach defences by the engineers, through to the heroic combat of the infantry battalions who stormed the German emplacements and went on to consolidate the beachhead.

A personal note: I was surprised, in reading the book, to realize how many of the decorated participants I knew. But then, closeted as we were on the Isle of Wight before the invasion — and often training in close quarters during the month leading up to D-Day — it is understandable that we should have become brothers-in-arms.

Bravo, too, for the excerpts in *Valour on Juno Beach* from the despatches of premier war correspondent Ross Munro and the extracts from the historical writings of Canadian War Historian Charles Stacey. I had worked with Ross Munro before the War in The Canadian Press. His monumental work, *Gauntlet to Overlord,* still stands as the best narrative of the Canadian assault on the Normandy beaches.

Years afterwards, Ross Munro was still asking the same question which the author quotes: "How did they do it?" Darned if I know.

Cliff Chadderton, OC, O.Ont., DCL, LLD
Captain, Royal Winnipeg Rifles
Chief Executive Officer,
The War Amputations of Canada.

Preface

The landing in Normandy, on 6 June 1944, was one of the great single events of the Second World War. Every Canadian soldier who participated in this action faced a situation which would test his courage and the skills he had been preparing for many years. This book is not a military history, but is a record of what happened to a number of Canadian soldiers, sailors and airmen in the summer of 1944.

From a practical point of view, only a small number of the men who landed could be formally recognized by an award for their actions. This book has been produced to present as complete a record as possible of all immediate awards made for gallantry on that day. Taken together, they depict the challenges faced and overcome by all ranks, branches and services. To better show the scope of these challenges, the citation for each award is given in the context of the historical events. Some periodic awards are included where these are relevant.

Each citation is presented with wording as close as possible to the original. Minor changes have been made only for style and grammar, or to provide a reasonable continuity with the preceding text. However, effort has been made to preserve the original text to the maximum, since this wording best conveys the emotions of what happened that day, fifty years ago.

Unfortunately, no easy single source is available to identify all the awards made on that day, but every effort has been made to examine all possible sources.

In addition, where citations dealt with several commendable acts, with only a brief reference to participation in D-Day, I have chosen, for the most part, to omit these in order to maintain the focus on this particular day. I must apologize to these individuals because of the limited scope of this work.

I would like to thank Dr W.A.B. Douglas, Director General History, Department of National Defence, and Hugh Halliday, of the Canadian War Museum, for identifying the naval and air force citations respectively.

T. Robert Fowler
Ottawa, 1994

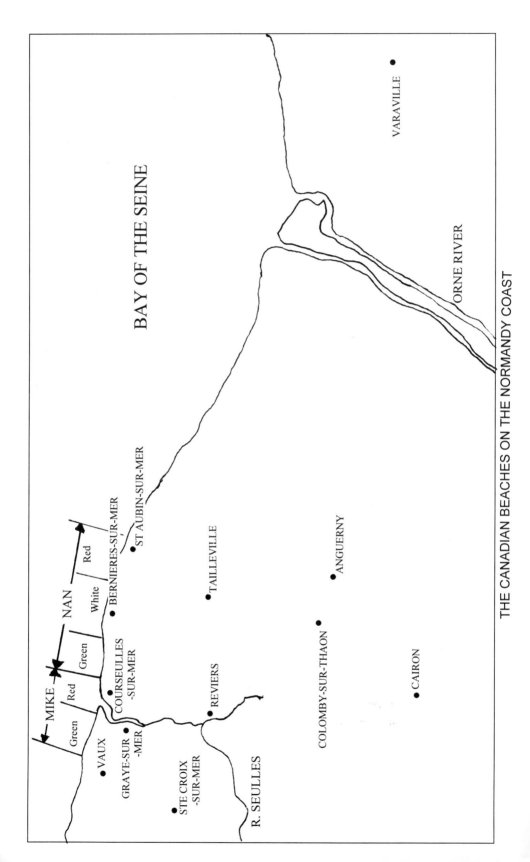

THE CANADIAN BEACHES ON THE NORMANDY COAST

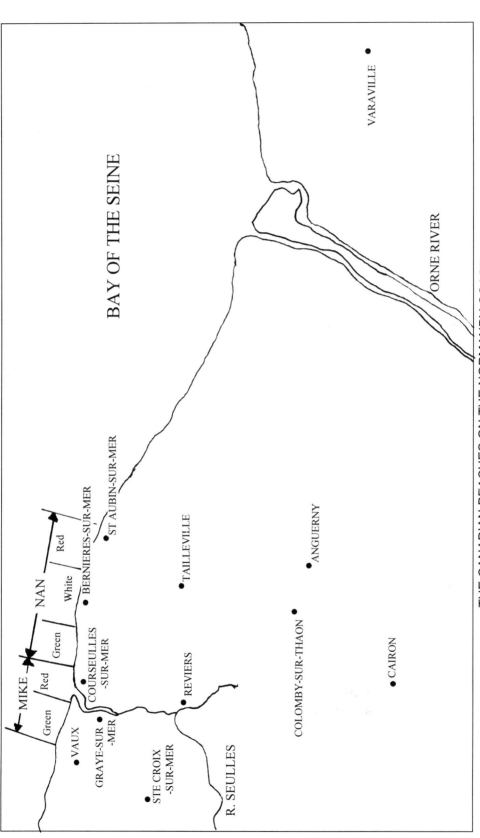

Introduction

On the 6th of June, 1944, assault troops of the 3rd Canadian Infantry Division, 2nd Canadian Armoured Brigade, and 1st Canadian Parachute Battalion, in conjunction with British and American forces, landed on the coast of France to begin the first step in the liberation of Europe. They carried with them an Order of the Day from General Dwight Eisenhower, Supreme Allied Commander:

> Soldiers, sailors and airmen of the Allied Expeditionary Forces! You are about to embark upon the great crusade, toward which we have striven these many months. The eyes of the world are upon you, the hopes and prayers of liberty-loving people everywhere march with you . . . [1]

On this day, the Canadian soldiers selected to be in the leading wave of this crusade felt the shock of coming to grips with the coastal defences which the Germans had been preparing for years. It would require great courage by all these men to leap from their swaying landing craft into water churned up by bullets and shells. Some would be recognized by awards for extraordinary courage. This book tells the story of D-Day in terms of the awards made for gallantry.

The focus of this book is on Juno Beach, as the title implies; however, an effort has been made to include any other major Canadian unit which was involved as part of the "great crusade", such as the 1st Canadian Parachute Battalion and the 29th Canadian Motor Torpedo Boat Flotilla.

---

1   David Eisenhower, Eisehower At War 1943 –1945 (New York: Random House Inc, 1986), p. 256.

THE CANADIAN FORCES

On Sunday, 10 September 1939, the Dominion of Canada declared that a state of war existed with the German Reich. The slide to war had been obvious for some time, however, and nine days earlier, the Department of National Defence had already authorized the immediate organization of an active service force of two divisions. The British government quickly asked Canada to come to its assistance by sending a token expeditionary force to England and, by late December, Winston Churchill announced to the world that the 1st Canadian Infantry Division had arrived.

This limited force of one division was all that the government of Mackenzie King had originally intended. However, events on the continent soon caused this concept to be revised. In early May 1940, the German armies broke through the French defences on the Meuse River and the British Expeditionary Force in Belgium was threatened with disaster. On 20 May 1940, the Canadian government announced the formation of the 3rd Division.[1]

In the organization of the 3rd Division, consideration was given to choosing units in such a way to ensure appropriate representation by all regions of the country. This is easily recognized by the make-up of the infantry brigades. The 7th Brigade was the "Western Brigade" - The Royal Winnipeg Rifles, Regina Rifles and the Canadian Scottish Regiment (from British Columbia). The 8th Brigade included the Queen's Own Rifles of Canada (from Toronto), the Régiment de la Chaudière (from the heart of Quebec), and the North Shore (New Brunswick) Regiment. The 9th Brigade was the "Highland Brigade", consisting of the Highland Light Infantry (from central Ontario), the Stormont, Dundas and Glengarry Highlanders (from Eastern Ontario), and the North Nova Scotia Highlanders. The machine-gun battalion was the Cameron Highlanders of Ottawa.

---

1   Col C.P. Stacey, *The Canadian Army 1939 - 1945* (Ottawa: King's Printer) p. 27.

The call to mobilize these regiments went out as the German armies threatened to destroy the British Expeditionary Force in northern France. The British troops managed miraculously to escape from Dunkirk but, in doing so, had to abandon their equipment. It was obvious that the war had taken a critical turn. In England, Canadian troops became the first line of defence. In Canada, Colonel C.P. Stacey recorded that, "in the emergency, the manhood of Canada came forward generously, eager to share the honour and peril of the moment with the men of the 1st Division . . . There was no difficulty in filling the ranks of the 3rd and 4th Divisions. The summer months of 1940 brought a flood of recruits . . . "[2]

On completion of mobilization in the autumn of 1940, the units of the 3rd Division began moving from all over the country to the Maritime provinces where they concentrated for basic training. In the summer of 1941, the division sailed for England. Soon after its arrival, the Division joined the rest of the Canadian Corps as it took over the defence of the south coast of Sussex. During 1942, increased emphasis began to be placed on offensive training, including training for amphibious assault. The Canadian forces in England were among the best trained and were eager for action. With the 1st Division slated to participate in the invasion of Sicily and the 2nd still recovering from the disaster of Dieppe, it was only natural that attention should turn to the 3rd Division. On 3 July 1943, it was officially announced that the 3rd Division had been selected for advanced assault training with a view to participating in the invasion of France, the operation code-named OVERLORD.[3]

Peter Simonds, a Canadian signals officer, has described the attitude of the men of the 3rd Division at this time:

> They were sometimes sneered at by the older arrivals as "new boys"; but when London and Washington picked the stellar Allied divisions for the D-Day assault role, the Third Canadian Division was the Canadian one selected.[4]

---

2   Col C.P. Stacey, *Six Years of War* (Ottawa: Queen's Printer, 1955) p. 30.

3   Col C.P. Stacey, *The Victory Campaign*(Ottawa: Queen's Printer, 1966) p. 34.

4   Peter Simonds, *Maple Leaf Up, Maple Leaf Down* (New York: Island Press, 1946) p. 19.

The German Army's lightning conquests in 1940 had caused the Allied high commands to finally wake up to the power of armoured warfare. The British War Office told Ottawa that they would like the Canadian Army to give priority to dispatching armoured units to England before further infantry. While Ottawa agreed to this request, there remained a controversy within the British Army as how best to organize their armoured forces. While some units were to be used for independent offensive action, others were designed to be primarily used for infantry support.

It was in this latter role that the 2nd Canadian Armoured Brigade was organized. As with the other major Canadian formations, its component units reflected the various regions of the country: the 6th Canadian Armoured Regiment (1st Hussars) from London, Ontario, the 10th Canadian Armoured Regiment (The Fort Garry Horse) from Winnipeg, Manitoba; and the 27th Armoured Regiment (The Sherbrooke Fusilier Regiment) from Quebec. In October 1943, the regiments were equipped with the latest Sherman tanks and came under the command of the 3rd Canadian Infantry Division to provide the vital tank support needed to break through the German coastal defences.

The third major unit selected to participate in the invasion was a unique unit — the 1st Canadian Parachute Battalion. In August 1940, Colonel E.L.M. Burns had proposed that a Canadian airborne unit should be formed. National Defence Headquarters was not initially in favour of such a move, but changed its mind in the summer of 1942. The battalion was created from volunteers, accepting only those who met very high standards. In early 1943, it was decided that the unit would be most effectively employed if it were part of a larger airborne force. As a result, the battalion sailed to join the new British 6th Airborne Division in July of 1943. As soon as they arrived in England, the Canadian paratroopers began training in preparation for OVERLORD.

But the plan for OVERLORD was to bring into play more than just the Army. As explained by Colonel C.P. Stacey:

> For once all three of the Canadian services [would fight] together. The 3rd Division held the centre of the stage; but overhead, the Canadian bombers of Number 6 Group and the fighter squadrons of Number 83 played their parts, as they had through the long months of preparation; while Canadian minesweepers helped to clear the way

across the turbulent Channel, and Canadian naval guns helped to beat down the enemy's defences. To the Army it was a particular source of delight that part of the 3rd Division was landed by craft of the Royal Canadian Navy.[5]

The Royal Canadian Navy, naturally, had a significant role. The naval assault force, which would transport the troops across the English Channel, included five Canadian landing craft flotillas totalling over thirty craft — the 260th, 262nd, 264th, 528th and 529th. The latter two flotillas were based on former luxury passenger steamships of the Canadian National Steamship Lines; the HMCS *Prince Henry* and the HMCS *Prince David*. These two ships, of about 6,000 tons, had been converted into their new military role after having been acquired by the Royal Canadian Navy early in the war. The Captain of the *Prince Henry*, Captain V.S. Godfrey, was designated senior officer of landing ships in Force J-1, thus responsible for discipline, navigation and station-keeping of the converted merchant vessels moving on Juno Beach[6].

The 31st Canadian Minesweeping Flotilla would assist in clearing some of the routes to the Allied beaches, and the fast craft of the 29th and 65th Motor Torpedo Boat Flotillas would patrol the flanks of the landing fleet's route. Finally, although only the destroyers HMCS *Sioux* and *Algonquin* would provide fire support on Juno Beach, Canadian destroyers and frigates would be present on other sectors. D-Day would thus be one of the high points in Canadian naval history, as argued by Brian Nolan:

> For a country on the eve of war whose navy's fleet consisted of two coal-burning minesweepers, six destroyers and a handful of harbour and patrol craft, she was now able to contribute 115 ships of the five thousand that made up the invasion fleet; as well, more than nine thousand Canadian sailors took part in Operation Neptune [the assault phase of OVERLORD].[7]

---

5   Stacey, *Victory*, p. 120.

6   Josph Schull, *Far Distant Ships* (Toronto: Stoddart Publishing Co. Ltd., 1987) p. 236.

7   Brian Nolan and Jeffrey Street, *Champagne Navy* (Toronto: Random House of Canada, 1991) p. 149.

OVERLORD —
THE INVASION OF FRANCE

For almost four years after the surrender of France, western Europe was held in the grip of one of the most brutal regimes the world has ever known. Nazi Germany enslaved the countries it conquered, drained their resources to the Reich's own end, and built a line of impressive defensive installations along the coast with the object of smashing any attempt by the British to return. But the Allied forces were determined to return and they gradually put together a plan for the cross-Channel assault, code-named OVERLORD.

The coast of Norman France was selected as the sector to be attacked. The plan called for a systematic destruction of all railways leading into the region over a period of many weeks as a result of attacks by both tactical and strategic air forces. During the night preceding the assault from the sea, three airborne divisions would be dropped inland, to seize key communications points and to disrupt the defenders from the rear. Among these forces would be the first Canadian participants in the invasion — the 1st Canadian Parachute Battalion whose task was to secure the easterly flank of Juno by occupying bridges over the River Orne and the high ground in that area.

Near first light on the day of the invasion, the seaborne landings would begin with five infantry divisions providing the shock troops - two American, two British and one Canadian. Prior to sunrise, the air forces would begin attacks on beach targets. A great fleet had been assembled to give powerful naval fire support to the infantry - seven battleships, 27 cruisers and 164 destroyers.[1] As the preliminary air bombing was ending, naval forces would open fire on more specific beach targets. Their fire would continue until the leading wave of landing craft had actually touched down on the beaches. Special equipment had been designed to give close fire support to the infantry as they came to grips with the actual defensive positions . The most important

---

[1]   Chester Wilmot, *The Struggle for Europe* (London: Collins, 1952) p. 180.

were DD (Duplex-Drive) tanks which could "swim" in and reach the beach at the same time as the infantry. Other specialized armoured vehicles had been built — "Flails", which could beat the ground with chains to explode mines, and Armoured Vehicles Royal Engineers (AVREs), which could place explosive charges to break open the concrete fortifications. With this vast scale, the OVERLORD plan was considered to be the most complex operation in military history.

The Canadian 3rd Infantry Division was assigned a four-and-a-half mile sector of the Normandy coast designated as "Juno" Beach, with a British division landing on either side of them. Juno was further sub-divided into sectors called "Mike" on the right and "Nan" on the left. The Canadian attack was to be made by the 7th and 8th Brigades, each with two battalions in the leading wave. On the extreme left, the North Shore Regiment was to assault the resort town of St Aubin-sur-Mer, with the Queen's Own Rifles to capture the adjoining beach town of Bernières-sur-Mer. They would be supported by tanks of the Fort Garry Horse. To their right, the Regina Rifles and Royal Winnipeg Rifles supported by tanks of the 1st Hussars were to land on either side of the little fishing town of Courseulles. A company of the Canadian Scottish was to assist the Royal Winnipeg Rifles by landing on the extreme right flank of the Canadian zone. Detachments of 3rd Division assault engineers would land with the infantry, carrying equipment to destroy beach obstacles and to clear paths through minefields at exits from the beaches. Finally, in addition to its own artillery components (the 12th, 13th and 14th Field Artillery Regiments), the Division was reinforced with the 19th Canadian Field Artillery Regiment so that each assaulting brigade would be supported by two artillery regiments.

Once the coastal objectives had been captured, the reserve battalions of the Division would land. Combined forces of infantry and tanks would then drive as hard as they could to reach their final objectives for the day, up to nine miles inland. The plan was ambitious, given the degree of violence with which the day would begin. But it had to be aggressive because, from past experience, the Allied commanders knew the Germans would react quickly.

These massive preparations were very necessary because the cross-Channel assault would be one of the riskiest operations of the war. In March 1942, anticipating that the Allies would make an attempt to carry out a large-scale invasion, Hitler ordered work to begin on the construction of the *Atlantikwall*.

This resulted in a chain of fortifications from Norway to the Spanish border. Coastal artillery batteries, encased in thick concrete casemates, resistant to even heavy bombs, were placed at strategic locations to engage Allied ships if they approached the coast. In the water, a maze of obstacles were placed to destroy any landing craft approaching the shore. On the beaches, concrete reinforced resistance nests were placed containing machine guns and anti-tank guns to destroy Allied infantry as they left their landing craft. Minefields and anti-tank ditches were placed to block the approaches to the pillboxes and trenches. Inland from the beaches, further resistance nests were located on any routes that Allied invaders would likely use.

Loading supplies on an LCI in Southampton Harbour.
NATIONAL ARCHIVES OF CANADA/ DND GM - 2102

There were four major resistance nests on Juno Beach, all containing one or more heavily concreted gun positions, well-protected by mines and barbed wire. The most easterly nest on the edge of the village of St. Aubin was based on a 50-mm anti-tank gun and four machine-guns, with an "exceptional command of the beach''. The next resistance nest at Bernières contained two 50-mm gun emplacements and seven machine-gun posts in front of the town along the sea-wall, which was from six to ten feet high. Guarding the harbour at Courseulles itself, the Germans had built their strongest position, designated as a more powerful strong point. Here, the eastern side of the harbour was covered by a casemated 88-mm and a 50-mm gun, while another casemated 75-mm gun was several hundred yards to the east. Another 75-mm and two 50-mm guns were located on the west side of the harbour entrance. Overall, the strongpoint contained twelve machine-gun posts. The last resistance nest at Vaux, on the westerly edge of Juno, contained another 75-mm gun in a concrete casemate.[2]

Loading supplies on an LCI in Southampton Harbour.
Copyright THE CANADIAN WAR MUSEUM.

2   Col C.P. Stacey, *The Victory Campaign* (Ottawa: Queen's Printer, 1955) 68-70;
     John Keegan, *Six Armies in Normandy* (London: William Collins and Sons, 1983) p. 89.

The weapons in these resistance nests were all carefully sited to fire along the beach, interlocking on the obstacles in the water. These obstacles varied in density along the invasion beach, but were sited to be submerged at high tide. They were set in the sand so that their sharpened points or the mines attached to them would destroy any landing craft approaching the shoreline. In the normal pattern used, the first rows in deepest water were made up of wooden or concrete stakes, pointing toward the sea. The next rows included "tetrahedra" (pyramid-shaped obstacles formed of three concrete, steel or wooden bars), and "hedgehogs" (obstacles made of three lengths of heavy angle-iron bolted together like a tripod). Finally, below the line of the high tide in front of Bernières and Courseulles, the Germans placed "C Elements", sections of massive steel anti-tank obstacles taken from Belgium's pre-war defences.

These and other defences along the Normandy coast made any landing difficult and dangerous. The ingenuity of the defences was largely due to Field Marshal Erwin Rommel who had been appointed commander of the armies in this sector in January 1944. From his battles in North Africa, he was well aware that the main Allied strength lay in its superiority in equipment, especially air power. He therefore argued that any Allied landing must be destroyed on the beaches: "We must stop him in the water, not only delaying him but destroying all his equipment while he is still afloat . . . The high water line must be the main fighting line."[3]

The Allied commanders also knew that the first hours were critical. Despite the great concentration of air and naval fire support, success still depended on the drive and determination of the few battalions of the leading wave touching down on dawn of the day of invasion. The leaders had seen what had happened at Dieppe. Even more recently, the Allied landing at Anzio in Italy had come close to failure. It worried Churchill. Early in 1943, when he was briefed on the developing plan for OVERLORD, Churchill shook his head and said, "I wake up at night and see the Channel floating with bodies of the cream of our youth."[4] He was worried about the losses and, for a time, sought an alternate strategy. But there was no other way.

---

3   Wilmot, p. 191.

4   Carlo D'Este. *Decision in Normandy* (London: William Collins and Sons, 1983) p. 89.

The Canadians were well aware of the dangers, but reacted in typical fashion. According to Peter Simonds:

> Men of the Third Canadian Division, wearing their pale blue (Prussian Grey) shoulder patches, became known to the rest of the Canadian Army as the 'death and glory boys', the 'charge of the light brigaders', etc., as D-Day neared. The Division's probable casualties on D-Day were variously calculated by experts at from 1,600 – 2,200. Some members of the Division remembered that the estimated 500 casualties for Dieppe had run to about seven times that figure and decided, on this basis, that they had just about "had it." But nothing seemed to upset or faze the morale of this magnificent body of men.[5]

The Atlantic Wall. The German defences along the coast included rows of deadly obstacles, exposed at low tide, backed by barbed wire and minefields on the beaches.
Painting by Capt. O. Fisher,Copyright THE CANADIAN WAR MUSEUM/12430.

---

5   Peter Simonds, *Maple Leaf Up, Maple Leave Down* (New York: Island Press, 1946), p. 129.

THE 6th OF JUNE —
ASSAULT FROM THE SKY

A storm battered the Channel coasts on the 5th of June, but Allied Meteorological staff predicted that, beginning on June 6th, a period of relative calm would last for thirty-six hours. The Supreme Allied Commander, General Eisenhower, made the decision that the invasion should proceed. Early that evening, ships anchored in safe harbours all along the south coast of England silently lifted anchor and moved out to join their allotted rendezvous points within a vast invasion armada of four thousand ships. At the same time, the engines of thousands of aircraft on airfields across southern England coughed into life.

Airborne Assault

Once the final decision had been taken to proceed with OVERLORD, the air forces and airborne troops were the first to move into action. The aircraft carrying these forces dramatically announced to the quiet English countryside that the invasion was on, as reported by a Canadian Spitfire pilot:

> During the early hours, most persons were awakened by a roar of planes overhead and the increased activity brought many from their beds. A great armada was passing overhead and by the light of the moon, which occasionally appeared between breaks in the cloud, we saw a scene to warm our hearts. There were heavy bombers and transport planes and behind each the outline of a glider. There were hundreds and they took over an hour to pass . . . the long line stretching across the sky as far as eye could see was one of the most magnificent and thrilling sights we had ever witnessed.[1]

1   *The RCAF Overseas: The Fifth Year* (Toronto: Oxford University Press), p. 225.

Several Canadian pilots were assigned to the Royal Air Force transport squadrons carrying the airborne forces.

Flight Lieutenant Norman Leslie Roseblade, RCAF, assigned to Number 190 Squadron, completed his first tour of duty as a navigator and took part in many sorties demanding a high standard of navigational ability in adverse weather. Now on his second tour of duty, he participated as a bombing leader in the D-Day operations in June 1944 and, later, in the airborne operations at Arnhem. In addition, Flight Lieutenant Roseblade flew on many missions to France, the Low Countries and Norway. Throughout his operational career, he displayed outstanding qualities of leadership and great devotion to duty.

For these actions, he was awarded the Distinguished Flying Cross.

Flying Officer Robert Sherlock Middleton, RCAF, assigned to Number 190 Squadron, completed a tour of operational duty which, at the end, included seventeen supply dropping missions to France, the Low Countries and Norway, and participation in the airborne landings at Normandy, Arnhem and the Rhine crossing. Throughout, as pilot and captain of aircraft, he displayed coolness and determination in the face of difficulties. [Flying Officer Middleton's citation describes further acts of courage under enemy fire during later missions.] At all times, Flying Officer Middleton's skill, cheerfulness and imperturbability have inspired the members of his crew with confidence.

For these actions, he was awarded the Distinguished Flying Cross.

Pilot Officer Jack Beauchamp Mutton, RCAF, assigned to Number 298 Squadron, completed two tours of operational duty. He flew over France, Belgium and Holland and made deep penetrations into Norway. This officer also towed gliders to Normandy, Arnhem and the Rhine crossing. At all times this officer accomplished his allotted tasks with skill and determination.

For these actions, he was awarded the Distinguished Flying Cross.

Squadron Leader William Hodgson Nickel, RCAF, assigned to Number 644 Squadron, participated in all the airborne operations in the Western European theatre of war including Normandy, Arnhem and the Rhine crossing. All these operations involved towing of gliders and on each occasion this officer brought his glider to the landing drome and successfully released it. He has proved to be a courageous and determined captain of aircraft and an inspiring flight commander.

For these actions, he was awarded the Distinguished Flying Cross.

Flight Lieutenant Vincent James Blake, RCAF, assigned to Number 644 Squadron, took part in all the airborne operations in the Western European Theatre of war including the landings in Normandy, and later at Arnhem and during the Rhine crossing. On all these occasions, the gliders towed by him have reached their destination successfully and discharged their troops safely. [Flight Lieutenant Blake's citation describes other actions later in the war, in one of which he was wounded.] He has at all times shown himself to be an officer of outstanding ability.

For these actions, he was awarded the Distinguished Flying Cross.

Warrant Officer David Henry Balmer, RCAF, assigned to Number 570 Squadron was a pilot of an aircraft detailed to transport and drop a force of paratroops whose role was to prepare and illuminate a landing zone for the use of later airborne forces representing a spearhead of the Allied invasion of Northern France. Much depended on the success of his important mission and the result obtained reflects the greatest credit on the skill and determination of this pilot. Warrant Officer Balmer completed several sorties and his example of keenness and devotion to duty was most commendable.

For his action, he was awarded the Distinguished Flying Cross.

At 2230 hours, 5 June, the "pathfinders" of the 6th British Airborne Division took off, their task to land by parachute and secure the "Drop Zone" where the bulk of the airborne forces would land. Among the pathfinders was "C" Company of the 1st Canadian Parachute Battalion. Their objective: to destroy the bridge over the Divette River and capture an enemy strong point at the village of Varaville.

"C" Company of the 1st Canadian Parachute Battalion
drop from the sky near Varaville. *Credit: David Craig.*

Because of poor navigation equipment and German anti-aircraft fire, the orderly course of some of the transport aircraft was disrupted and many men of "C" Company were dispersed over a wide area. As a result, only about thirty-eight men managed to rendezvous near Varaville. Despite the numerically superior German force in a well-fortified position containing a 75-mm gun, Major H.M. MacLeod led his men "into Varaville and first attacked and captured the big chateau which was the officers' mess for the German H.Q. They were fired on heavily by a German anti-tank gun and machine-guns."[2] The return German fire mortally wounded Major MacLeod. Captain J.P. Hanson arrived just as this happened and "Major MacLeod died in Captain Hanson's lap a few minutes later." Captain Hanson took over to continue the offensive action, with the result that, shortly after 1000 hours, the Germans surrendered to the thirty remaining Canadians.

2   Ross Munro, *Gauntlet to Overlord* (Toronto: The Macmillan Company of Canada, 1945), p. 127.

Captain John Philip Hanson of the 1st Canadian Parachute Battalion receiving the Military Cross from General Bernard L. Montgomery, Commander-in-Chief of the Allied ground forces in Normandy. *NATIONAL ARCHIVES OF CANADA/PA-191065.*

At Varaville, on 6 June 44, in an attack on a strongly fortified position, Captain John Philip Hanson's company commander was killed. Captain Hanson immediately took over command and, showing exceptional leadership and courage, attacked the position inflicting casualties and taking forty prisoners. He immediately consolidated this position and held it under enemy mortar fire until relieved. Captain Hanson was wounded in this action but continued to command his company.

For this action, he was awarded the Military Cross.

As part of this action, Private William Ducker, of the 1st Canadian Parachute Battalion, was a medical orderly attached to "C" Company. The Company commander, a platoon commander and two Canadian other ranks were in a building being heavily engaged by an anti-tank gun and mortar. A direct hit caused all four to become casualties. Private Ducker, with absolute disregard for his own safety under heavy machine-gun and mortar fire, went to this building which was still under heavy fire, gave medical attention to the Company commander and ascertained that the others were dead or beyond medical aid before removing the Company commander to a place of safety which was also under heavy fire.

For this action, he was awarded the Military Medal.

By midday, June 6, the 1st Canadian Parachute Battalion had successfully carried out all the tasks assigned to it in Operation OVERLORD.

The Tactical Air Support

Thirty minutes before H Hour, the Allied tactical air forces began to attack the German beach defences along all the landing beaches. On the British-Canadian front, this support was provided by the RAF's 2nd Tactical Air Force, whose Number 83 Group contained fifteen RCAF squadrons along with an RCAF reconnaissance wing of three squadrons.

On Juno Beach, "Squadron Leader H.H. Norsworthy's Westmount [Number 439 Fighter Bomber] Typhoon Squadron bombed gun positions at Courseulles in support of 3rd Canadian Infantry Division. Diving through billowing clouds of smoke and debris hurled up by the intense naval bombardment, the pilots attacked two enemy batteries . . . In the afternoon, as the three Typhoon squadrons made armed reconnaissances of the area around Caen, they bombed roads along which armoured cars and trucks were moving [and later] surprised a long armoured column . . . seriously damaging at least a score of vehicles."[3]

On this day, RCAF Number 414 Squadron, specializing in fighter reconnaissance duties, would particularly distinguish itself.

Flight Lieutenant Lewis Farnell May of Number 414 RCAF Squadron completed many sorties against the enemy and, as a reconnaissance pilot, continuously displayed exceptional skill and courage in completing the many

---

3   *RCAF Overseas*, p. 227.

tasks assigned to him, frequently in the face of the most intense enemy opposition. He has also attacked a variety of ground targets in enemy occupied territory. On the first day of the assault on the coast of Normandy, this officer performed two very successful co-operation flights in support of the naval bombardment.

For these actions, he was awarded the Distinguished Flying Cross.

Flight Lieutenant Gordon Wonnacott of Number 414 RCAF Squadron completed a large number of operational sorties of low level photography and tactical reconnaissance. In the initial stages of the liberation of Normandy, this officer twice flew long sorties directing naval bombardment. His day intruder activities resulted in the destruction of two enemy aircraft and numerous trains and barges damaged. He showed exceptional keenness and devotion to duty throughout a long period and set a magnificent example to all. He was an outstanding officer who showed great qualities of leadership as a flight commander.

For his actions, he was awarded the Distinguished Flying Cross.

Flight Lieutenant James Robert Macelwain of Number 2 Squadron successfully completed numerous low level photographic sorties and tactical reconnaissance missions. In the course of these operations, he inflicted considerable damage on the enemy's river transport, trains and mechanical transport and destroyed two flying bombs. His aircraft was hit on seven occasions but he never let either enemy opposition or adverse weather deter him from completing his mission. At dawn on D-Day, Flight Lieutenant Macelwain completed several naval bombardment shots for more than two hours at low level over the French coast despite continuous anti-aircraft fire. He neutralized three guns and only returned to base through lack of fuel. Soon after landing, this officer took off again and flew another two hours over the heavily defended coast where he neutralized more enemy guns. Throughout his operational career this officer displayed a high standard of efficiency and a fine fighting spirit.

For his actions, he was awarded the Distinguished Flying Cross.

THE 6th OF JUNE —
ASSAULT FROM THE SEA

Infantry Landing Ship's, "Q" boats and a minesweeper of the assault fleet shortly after dawn on D-Day morning, as seen from the port beam of HMCS Prince David.
NATIONAL ARCHIVES OF CANADA/DND PD-367.

As soon as the decision for OVERLORD had been taken, the 31st Canadian Minesweeping Flotilla was ordered to sea. Their task, along with nine other flotillas containing six additional Canadian minesweepers, was to sweep the eight-mile deep German minefields leading to one of the American landing sectors, called Omaha Beach. It was slow and laborious work but, at the same time, nerve-wracking, since they would be within range of the German coastal batteries at Point Barfleur. At 0515 hours, June 6, they completed the last of their work, surprisingly without any German reaction, and met the first of the assault ships coming into the channels.[1]

Acting Commander Anthony Hubert Gleadow Storrs, was in command of the 31st Minesweeping Flotilla of the Sweeper Group which swept the various channels necessary to ensure the safe approach of the main Assault Force to its pre-determined position off the coast of France. Acting Commanding Storrs swept and marked these channels in enemy-mined waters, under cover of darkness, in a cross tide and during adverse conditions of weather. His courage, skill and sound judgment displayed in the execution of this complex and difficult operation signalled his resourcefulness and outstanding ability, and contributed materially to the success of the operation.

For this action, he was awarded a Bar to the Distinguished Service Cross and the American Legion of Merit.[2]

As the airborne forces and bombers were taking off, the naval convoys were cutting through the waters of the English Channel. The men on board soon found the weather still far from ideal. As Ross Munro described it:

Out on deck the wind howled through the wireless masts which spouted profusely from the upper deck. The sky was black as the inside of a gun barrel and spray and rain lashed the deck. It was a terrible night for the crossing. The sea seemed worse than ever and the ship creaked and groaned as she ploughed her way through it.[3]

The War Diary of the Royal Winnipeg Rifles describes the beginning of their day:

0400   Tea and a cold snack was served as breakfast to all in the Battalion. Few were able to keep their meals down due to the rough sea. Patiently, each [rifleman] waited his serial section to be called to board his respective landing craft. As each

---

1   Joseph Schull, *Far Distant Ships* (Toronto: Stoddart Publishing Co Ltd, 1950), p. 267-272.

2   Hal Lawrence, *Victory At Sea* (Toronto: McClelland & Stewart Inc., 1989) p. 295.

3   Ross Munro, *Gauntlet to Overlord*, (Toronto: Macmillan Company of Canada, 1945) p. 53.

H/Captain Robert Seaborn, padre of the Canadian Scottish Regiment, leads some of his men in prayer just before embarking on their landing craft. For his actions later that day, Captain Seaborn was awarded the Croix de Guerre.
NATIONAL ARCHIVES OF CANADA/PA-129054.

group was called the tension mounted. Somehow the minutes passed and all was ready.

0515 All LCAs [Landing Craft Assault] were now manned and lowered into the turbulent English Channel. Still 10 miles from shore, the tiny crafts bobbed up and down as they piled their way forward in the rough sea. Only the hardiest rifleman was able to keep his stomach in check and not reach for his vomit bag.

0655 The Invasion Fleet opposite Juno Beach had been in sight of the beach for nearly three hours and the enemy had still to fire a shot. Precisely at 0655, the Royal Navy and the landing craft carrying the self-propelled guns of the 3rd Canadian Division

Landing Craft Assault craft heading into shore.
NATIONAL ARCHIVES OF CANADA/DND A-639.

opened fire on the enemy's shore defences. "Everything from cruisers to landing craft carrying rockets fired salvo after salvo into the enemy targets . . . "[4]

The assaulting infantry were transported across the Channel in large Landing Ships, Infantry (LSIs), on which the assault landing craft (LCAs) were carried. When these ships reached their designated launching positions off the French coast, the LCAs were lowered into the sea and the infantry clambered on board. The LCAs headed in, with the plan to touch down five minutes after H-hour by which time, it was hoped, the advance engineers would have cleared a satisfactory number of the beach obstacles.[5]

4   Bruce Tascona and Eric Wells, *Little Black Devils* (Winnipeg: Frye Publishing, 1983) p. 144-145.

5   Col C. P. Stacey, *The Victory Campaign* (Ottawa: The Queen's Printer, 1966), p. 102.

On the Canadian front, two Canadian LCA flotillas participated in the landing - 528th from the HMCS *Prince Henry* and the 529th from the HMCS *Prince David*. Joseph Schull has described the approach of the LCAs to the shore:

> The assault flights deployed from line ahead to line abreast a few hundred yards off MIKE and NAN beaches . . . *Prince Henry*'s flotilla charged in through the surf before MIKE RED, and the awful quiet which had seemed to possess the beaches in contrast to the roar of the bombardment was again broken by mortar and machine-gun fire, the crash of boats tearing out their bottoms on obstacles, and the bursts of exploding mines.

> LCA 856 crashed sideways into one of the concrete pyramids, swerved off, surged up the beach. LCA 1021, racing in beside a tank landing craft, collided with the larger vessel and was heaved broadside onto shore . . . [Among the larger landing craft, Craft 121 crashed into an obstacle] which stopped her dead, holed its forward space and killed or wounded nine soldiers . . . 250 had her nose blown off by a mine.[6]

Lieutenant J.C. Davie, RCNVR, commanding officer of 528th Royal Canadian Navy LCA Flotilla, displayed outstanding leadership and skill when, despite heavy enemy fire, rough seas, and mined obstacles, successfully took charge of the beaching of all his LCAs and brought them back to the ship, with the exception of one which had been blown up by a mine. Two of these craft were in sinking condition and it is mostly due to this officer's skill and leadership that they, and their crews, were got safely back to the ship.

For his actions, he was awarded the Distinguished Service Cross, "for good service during the invasion of Normandy."

At approximately 0820 hours, off the village of Bernières-sur-Mer, Lieutenant James Edward Whittaker of the 5th Canadian Field Company RCE was in a landing craft coming in on the assault wave, when it struck the outer row of obstacles and came to a halt in over eight feet of water at the ramp.

---

6   Schull, p. 278-279.

Small arms fire was being brought to bear on the craft. The craft attempted to get closer to shore with no appreciable results. Lieutenant Whittaker finally decided that he must get ashore in order to contact the other sections and see what work could be done on the beach. He attempted to swim ashore, knowing that he was not a good swimmer and knowing that fire would be directed upon him. He failed to make the shore and was brought back to the craft in a state of near drowning. In the meantime, the craft had worked its way into the shore, and the bulldozers and men commenced to disembark. At this time, splinters from mortar fire struck Lieutenant Whittaker on the face and neck, preventing him from disembarking. Before he had sufficiently recovered from the shock of his wounds and near drowning, he insisted that he be brought inshore again and be allowed to disembark. He rejoined his platoon at approximately 1:30 p.m. and worked on obstacle removing and road clearance until 10:30 p.m. that night when he was in a state of complete exhaustion.

By his devotion to duty and refusal to quit under most adverse conditions, this officer succeeded in carrying out many hours of useful work before he allowed himself to relax.

Captured German Strong Point. The anti-tank gun at St Aubin-sur-Mer.
Painted by Capt. O. Fisher, THE CANADIAN WAR MUSEUM, 12438.

In the weeks prior to D-Day, Lieutenant Whittaker had been outstanding in his efforts to train his men to the highest peak of efficiency and was instrumental in bringing out many new ideas and methods in underwater obstacle removal.

For this action, he was awarded the Military Cross.

Red Beach of Nan Sector

The men of the North Shore Regiment leaped out of their landing craft at 0740 hours and were met by heavy fire — the resistance nest and the large concrete gun shelter at St Aubin had not been touched by the preliminary bombardment. Lieutenant McCann of "B" Company wrote:

> Things weren't going as planned and unless we captured those heavy guns Jerry was potting landing craft with, things were going to get worse. And worse they got, for there we were with nothing heavier than Brens with which to attack heavily-fortified enemy posts.[7]

Major Robert Borden Forbes commanded "B" Company, the left assault company of the North Shores. On landing, he found that the strong point commanding this beach was more strongly held than had been anticipated and he also realized during the "run-in" that certain portions of the "softening-up" fire support was not forthcoming. Despite these very material setbacks, this officer through his coolness, initiative and determination fought his company through to their objective and finally seized the strong point and its many fire points. Had this portion of the beach not been captured, the landing of many serials would have been very costly. His personal display of cool bravery and decision held his company together as a fire team.

For this action, he was awarded the Military Cross.

Corporal Frederick Stanley Savage was a section leader in No. 2 Platoon, "A" Company of the North Shores. Shortly after landing, Corporal Savage was cut off from his platoon and came under heavy mortar fire in the beach area. Corporal Savage had no way of knowing the fate of the remainder of his

---

7   Will R. Bird, *North Shore (New Brunswick) Regiment* (Brunswick Press, 1983) p. 201.

platoon or of his company, but he realized the importance of capturing the platoon objective. He quickly rallied his section and led them under intense mortar fire to the attack and capture of the platoon objective. In this attack, his section had to clear a number of houses which were sown with booby traps and mines and held by the enemy. In spite of these handicaps, Corporal Savage fought through to his objective and employed his section to hold it. He then reported to company headquarters that the objective had been captured. Throughout this operation, Corporal Savage showed unflinching determination to carry out his commander's intention. His present personal courage was an example to his men at all times and inspired them to the successful completion of a difficult task.

For this action, he was awarded the Military Medal.

As these events were going on, Number 4 Platoon, under Lieutenant C.F. Richardson was in trouble:

Tracer bullets from German anti-aircraft seemed to fill the air as we came in . . . Once we were out of the boat everyone acted mechanically, heading for the beach and the cover of the beach wall . . . we used our bangalore torpedoes with good effect and were at close quarters with the enemy after traversing through what we later discovered was a mine field. The Germans were back of concrete and we were without armoured support. Soon the sniping became the most demoralizing aspect of the day as we began to lose one man after another."[8] At this point, Private Harry Blakely moved to get help by crossing an open area swept by machine-gun fire.

Private Harry Wellington Blakely of the North Shore Regiment's "B" Company brought vital information concerning his platoon to his company commander stating than they were pinned down by mortar and machine-gun fire and that they could neither advance or withdraw. If some supporting fire could not be obtained, the platoon would be completely wiped out. To do this, Private Blakely had to cross an open area swept by enemy machine-gun fire

---

8   Bird, p. 202.

which he did with complete disregard to his own personal safety. Private Blakely then returned to his platoon with information that assistance could be given to them. Having cooly completed his task, he went to the section with the greatest number of casualties and immediately rendered assistance to the wounded, removing them to a safer area. His coolness, initiative and bravery saved the lives of many of his comrades in his platoon.

For this action, he was awarded the Military Medal.

Lieutenant Richardson described the situation:
the company commander "was able to get the tanks in action for us and none too soon as we had lost seventeen men, dead and wounded, from the sniping and shelling." For Lieutenant Richardson's platoon, it was fortunate that the amphibious tanks of "C" Squadron of the Fort Garry Horse had made their way in through the heavy waves in good time.

Major William Roy Bray commanded the special assault tanks of "C" Squadron of the Fort Garry Horse, and was one of the first to land in the area of St Aubin. He got his squadron ashore against a very heavy sea and in the face of strong enemy fire. On landing, he found that the enemy mine fields were holding up the advance and the resulting congestion would prejudice the success of the operation. He immediately led his squadron across the mine field and, at the cost of three of his tanks, was able to restore the situation and support the infantry into St Aubin. With outstanding skill and personal courage, he controlled the fire and movement of his troops in such a manner as to best support the assault infantry onto their objective. He did this successfully despite considerable loses in tanks an crews.

The commander of the assault infantry considered that the aggressive action of this squadron had the greatest effect upon their successful seizing of beach positions. He extolled the bravery and coolness of the squadron leader during the action. His actions on D-Day were outstanding and his personal bravery and aggressive leadership was an inspiration to his troops. The support provided the assault infantry by this Squadron undoubtedly contributed largely to the success of the day's accomplishments.

For this action, he was awarded the Distinguished Service Order.

Sergeant Harley Walterson, a tank crew commander of the Fort Garry Horse, observed the strong point in particular and, on his own initiative and in the face of heavy fire, directed his troop onto it. This action resulted in the silencing of a 75-mm gun which was causing great trouble; some thirty of the enemy were killed and upwards of one hundred others surrendered. It was owing to his coolness, courage and skill that the strong point was knocked out, thus enabling our infantry to gain their immediate objective. His actions are worthy of the highest commendation.

For this action, he was awarded the Military Medal.

In the meantime, with the beach area under continuing heavy fire, first aid men coming to the aid of the wounded were in a very dangerous situation. Private Adair of the North Shore Regiment described the situation:

Of the three stretcher bearers with "A" Company, one was wounded and two were killed. That left me. We wore the Red Cross armband until the first man got killed, then we took them off. The Germans were using them as targets.[9]

Private Robert William Adair was attached as a Stretcher Bearer to "A" Company during the attack. The three other Stretcher Bearers became casualties in the early stages, and Private Adair rendered First Aid to the casualties of the entire company. Although the beach was under fire and mined, he rendered First Aid to the injured with little or no regard for his personal safety.

When he had finished his work on the beach, he moved into the village to attend to the wounded there, with complete disregard to his own safety. He went among booby traps around the buildings after being warned of them and moved among the injured rendering First Aid. Throughout the remainder of the day and into the night, Private Adair moved among the wounded and treated them until his supplies were exhausted.

---

9   A.R. Byers, ed., *The Canadians At War 1939/45* (Westmount: The Reader's Digest, 1986) p. 327.

His courage and devotion to duty were an inspiration to all the company. His cool display of valour far beyond the ordinary call of service helped to inspire his comrades on to accomplish deeds which otherwise might have proved impossible.

For this action, he was awarded the Military Medal.

Stretcher-Bearers of the North Shore Regiment in St Aubin-sur-Mer.
CREDIT/David Craig.

Captain John Aubry Patterson was the North Shore Regiment's Medical Officer, landing with Battalion Headquarters and the reserve companies of the North Shore Regiment. His work under fire was exemplary. As long as the Regimental Stretcher Bearers were available to 'nest' or carry injured men, he went from 'nest' to 'nest', administering all the aid within his resources in a cool and capable manner without any apparent regard for the shelling, mortaring and small arms fire falling around him. When the Stretcher Bearers themselves became very reduced in numbers, he attempted to reach each individual until Battalion Headquarters and the Regimental

Aid Post were moved inland. Here he carried on for the next thirty-six hours without respite despite persistent sniping and shelling.

Finally, an instance of his conduct under fire was the occasion when he walked deliberately into a concentration of medium artillery fire to render assistance to the wounded in the vicinity of the church at Cairon.

Due to the very faithful and courageous manner in which Captain Patterson performed his work, the number of lives lost amongst those wounded was very much lower than might easily have been the case.

For this action, he was awarded the Military Cross.

During this time, *Lieutenant John Leonard Heaslip was in command of a section of the 22nd Canadian Field Ambulance which landed in support of the North Shore Regiment. Immediately on landing, it was necessary to collect and render first aid to the casualties. Enemy mortar and machine-gun fire was heavy and continuous. Lieutenant Heaslip rallied his section and directed their efforts in collecting and nesting casualties in what little shelter was offered by the sea wall on the beach. With complete disregard for his own personal safety, he made frequent sorties to the most exposed parts of the beach to render aid and to bring the casualties into shelter. Throughout the entire assault until the North Shore Regiment reached* their final objective, *this officer by his gallantry, initiative and leadership was an inspiration to his men.*

For this action, he was awarded the Military Cross.

Corporal Douglas Bertram MacDonald was another member of the 22nd Canadian Field Ambulance on the beach, engaged with his section in collecting and treating casualties. Mortar and machine-gun fire was heavy and continuous. Several casualties were seen to occur at the east end of the beach wall. On his own initiative and with complete disregard for his own personal safety, Corporal MacDonald collected three stretcher bearers and crawled thirty yards to render First Aid to these casualties. While so engaged, a mortar shell exploded a few feet from them, killing two of the bearers, wounding the third and severely wounding Corporal MacDonald about the face. Still conscious, but blinded, he retained presence of mind and attempted to crawl to the shelter of the sea wall. He was removed and treated by other members of the section. Throughout the entire action until becoming a casualty, Corporal MacDonald showed complete fearlessness and great initiative and leadership. His conduct was in every way an inspiration to the men in his section.

Wounded Canadian soldiers of the 8th Brigade, collected on the beach, awaiting removal to a Casualty Clearing Station.
D.I. Grant/ NATIONAL ARCHIVES OF CANADA/ PA-132384

For this action, he was awarded the Military Medal.

Padre Hickey was among those landing, sharing in the trials met by the men under his care. Will Bird wrote: "That hero, Padre Hickey, jumped into the water with Joe Murray and waded ashore, saw the lad next to him fall, dragged him ashore and anointed him - the first of a long, long list.[10]

---

10   Bird, p. 231.

H/Captain Raymond Myles Hickey, Canadian Corps of Chaplain Services (RC), had been the Padre of the North Shore Regiment since the battalion had been mobilized. He accompanied the Battalion Headquarters in the reserve company wave in the assault on the beach of St Aubin-sur-Mer at H plus 20 minutes on the 6th of June, 1944. Captain Hickey rendered first aid to the wounded and spiritual comfort to the dying without any apparent regard for his own safety. In one instance, two men hit by mortar fragments stumbled into and fell amongst a number of booby traps and mines. Although warned, Captain Hickey went into the field, applied first aid, and returned with these men despite the fact that fire on this exposed area was heavy. On another occasion, when stretcher bearers were called for, the Padre walked up and exposed himself as the quickest means of getting to the wounded men, again despite the cross fire. Having rendered first aid, he managed to make these men as comfortable and safe as the circumstances permitted, and then walked across the beach to a light section of the Field Ambulance, RCAMC, to notify them of the location of the wounded.

This conduct, courageous, effective and without thought of personal safety, was an inspiration to all ranks. Even in the strife and strain of our baptism of fire, our admiration for our Padre was further heightened.

For these actions, he was awarded the Military Cross.

Clearing the obstacles and mines was one of the key tasks to be done on landing. Because some of the landings occured later than planned, and the tide was rising faster than predicted, clearing the obstacles became more difficult than expected. In addition, the continuing heavy enemy fire made the work of the engineers very hazardous.

Company Sergeant Major (CSM) Seymour Wylde Howes of the 16th Field Company RCE was in a Landing Craft Infantry (L) coming in one hour after the infantry touched down. His boat, with thirty-four men of Number 1 Platoon of the 16th Canadian Field Company, Royal Canadian Engineers (RCE), struck a mine when it was one hundred yards offshore of Nan Red Beach, and grounded in ten feet of water. CSM Howes and several men made their way ashore and immediately afterwards a life line was passed to the beach to assist the remaining personnel. On two occasions, CSM Howes plunged back into the water to assist drowning men ashore. Corporal

Creighton of Number 1 Platoon later stated that he would not have reached the beach without CSM Howes' assistance. All this time, enemy snipers were continually firing on the beaches and, by leaving the security of the sea wall and going back into the water, CSM Howes stood considerable risk of being shot and drowned. He performed these deeds regardless of his own safety.

For these actions, he was awarded the Military Medal.

Major Frank Alexander McTavish, commanding the 5th Canadian Field Company RCE, was responsible for clearance of underwater obstacles. He landed with one of this platoons at H Hour on Nan Red Beach at St Aubin-sur-Mer. His craft grounded on something, with about ten feet of water at the ramp, under small arms fire from the beach. Determined to get ashore and get started with his task, he arranged for tow ropes from the bulldozers for the personnel to hold on to and also one to tow his 5 cwt truck. Lieutenant Stalker was killed instantly, and the 5 cwt tow rope parted.

Major McTavish and his men reached the shore and started clearance of obstacles but, due to heavy small arms fire and the height of water, this was impossible.

At that time, four tanks, hull down at the water's edge, were hit and started to burn. Major McTavish's party suffered heavily while trapped between the exploding tanks and the fire from the enemy positions on shore.

His Number 46 radio set was lost coming in, so his only means of establishing communications with the platoon next to him was by personal contact. After two unsuccessful attempts, he managed to scale the low cliff and get around to his next platoon and to the Principal Beach Master (PBM). After discussion with the PBM, it was decided where the priority work of obstacle clearing would start and Major McTavish organized this, remaining on the job until some 1800 yards of beach was cleared.

From the time that underwater obstacles were first known to exist on their front, 5th Canadian Field Company was given the task of dealing with them. Major McTavish's keen interest in the work reflected all through the Company and the result was that they were at all times quite sure of themselves and their ability to cope with what they might find. The working out of all drills and the calculation and design of the shaped charges used was all done under his supervision and guidance.

For these actions, he was awarded the Distinguished Service Order.

Lance/Corporal Harold Joseph Bartolacci was another engineer of the 16th Canadian Field Company RCE who landed on Nan Red Beach. He found that the enemy had placed a steel rail across the exit road from the beach, thus blocking it for our tanks. Although this obstacle was fully covered by enemy small arms fire, Lance/Corporal Bartolacci dashed forward, under covering fire from our own troops, placed a charge and destroyed the obstacle. This act of gallantry enabled the tanks to move forward and assist the infantry in their advance.

For this action, he was awarded the Military Medal.

At approximately 0900 hours, Lance/Sergeant Alexander Finnie Killah was proceeding down the beach at the extreme left of Nan Red Beach, searching for the remainder of his section when he came upon a blazing Sherman tank which was exploding intermittently because of the shells and mines carried inside. Lance/Sergeant Killah noticed a soldier lying beside the track of the tank apparently dead but, on further scrutiny, noticed movement. Killah and Sapper Coveyduck ran to the side of this tank, disregarding the very great danger of this tank exploding at any moment, as well as aimed enemy small arms fire. He placed this wounded man on the stretcher and, with the help of Sapper Coveyduck, bore him to safety.

For this action, he was awarded the Military Medal.

At 30 minutes past H Hour on D-Day, Sapper Walter Richard Coveyduck of the 5th Canadian Field Company RCE was in a position on the seaward side of the sea wall on the extreme left of Nan Red Beach taking cover from enemy fire from a position on the left flank. An LCI (L) touched down immediately in front of Sapper Coveyduck's position and lowered its ramps. Infantry commenced to disembark but the leaders were shot down. At the same time, the action of the surf turned over the starboard ramp, which then became entangled with the port ramp, preventing the remainder of the infantry from disembarking. Sapper Coveyduck, seeing the perilous position of the remainder of the troops on board the craft, with the great presence of mind, disregarding enemy small arms fire, ran to the craft and disentangled the ramps. He turned the port ramp right side up, anchoring it to the ground with his own weight, at the same time shouting and waving to the infantry on board to get off quickly. He remained with the ramp until the infantry commenced to disembark.

Approximately half an hour after the above incident, Sapper Coveyduck was accompanying Lance/Sergeant Killah in the latter's search for the remainder of his section, when they came upon a blazing Sherman tank which was filled with shells and mines. A soldier was laying prone beside the tank and Lance/Sergeant Killah and Sapper Coveyduck noticed movement of his body. Completely disregarding the danger from this exploding and blazing tank, and also enemy aimed small arms fire, Sergeant Killah and Sapper Coveyduck picked up a stretcher, ran to the side of the tank, placed the wounded man on the stretcher, and took him out of danger.

For these actions, he was awarded the Distinguished Conduct Medal.

Sergeant Hugh Morris Fitzpatrick was a non-commissioned officer of the 5th Canadian Field Company RCE in charge of the special beach obstacle clearance party of the landing on the Normandy coast. He was unaccompanied by an officer and landed at H hour. Even though the obstacles were still under very heavy fire from the beaches, he and his men, encouraged by his example, worked at great personal risk to themselves and carried out their dangerous task with above average success. He continued his task after the departure of the enemy and very rapidly disposed of the remaining mined obstacles. This NCO's devotion to duty contributed much towards the success of the operation and he should receive recognition.

For these actions, he was awarded the Military Medal.

D-Day Assault. The landing of the Queen's Own Rifles of Canada at Bernières-sur-Mer.
Credit: THE QUEEN'S OWN RIFLES of CANADA.

White Beach of Nan Sector

Lieutenant-Colonel W.T. Barnard described the struggle that the Queen's Own Rifles of Canada had to the west of the North Shores:

> "A" Company on the right and "B" Company on the left touched down at 0812 hours. The line between the companies was the railway station. Several L.C.A. hit mines on the run in but casualties were light . . . The rising tide had now left about two hundred yards or so of the beach between the water's edge and the sea-wall. The strip was swept by enemy enfilade fire but, with a rush, "A" Company, under Major H.E. Dalton, was over; clambered up the sea-wall, and reached the railway line.[11]

Major Hume Elliot Dalton, commanding "A" Company of the Queen's Own Rifles, personally led his men ashore against the German strong points.

---

11   Lt-Col W.T. Barnard, *Queen's Own Rifles of Canada 1860-1960* (Don Mills: The Ontario Publishing Co., 1960) p. 194.

So fierce was the attack of "A" Company, that the German resistance was quickly overcome. Still at the head of his men, Major Dalton led them through the town of Bernières, driving the enemy into the fields beyond. So quickly and with so much dash was his task completed, the reserve companies were able to land without a shot being fired at them from the beach defences.

For this action, he was awarded the Distinguished Service Order.

However, on the extreme right flank, 9 Platoon of "A" Company of the Queen's Own Rifles received heavy casualties from an 88-mm gun position which had not been identified by air photographs.

Number 9 Platoon had been detailed to knock out a supposed machine-gun post on the right of the company. Shortly after the platoon was committed to this action, Sergeant Charles William Smith's platoon commander became a casualty and was knocked out of the fight. The platoon itself suffered severe casualties, being pinned down by heavy mortar and machine-gun fire. Sergeant Smith, although himself wounded, showed great leadership and ability by laying down return fire and rendering what turned out to be a strongly held position ineffective against the landing of other troops on the beaches. He organized his platoon until its fire neutralized effectively the fire of the enemy position. Had he not done so it would have been impossible to land the next company on the beach at this point. When his platoon was finally relieved he led it back to the company rendezvous and stayed in action until ordered to report for medical treatment by his company commander. His actions throughout were an inspiration to all ranks.

For this action, he was awarded the Military Medal.

Meanwhile, "B" Company of the Queen's Own Rifles had experienced an even more difficult landing.

The company had landed directly in front of a concrete strongpoint that was still in action. Almost one half of the company was lost in the initial dash across the beach. A supporting flak ship was wirelessed for support. The flak ship came in so close that it almost ran aground and began firing at point-blank range.[12]

---

12   Barnard, p. 195.

Major Charles Osborne Dalton commanded "B" Company in the assault. This Company was met by severe machine-gun fire from an enemy strong point immediately to its front. Despite the fact that heavy casualties were being suffered in the landing craft from mines and obstacles and, that in the first few minutes after landing, there were sixty-five casualties, Major Dalton led his men forward across the beach to assault the position. Although severely wounded in the head on first landing, he continued to lead his men and personally was instrumental in knocking out one of the pillboxes. By this officer's example of leadership and bravery, and his coolness in the face of stiff opposition, the enemy fortified position was quickly overrun, and the company which followed in the landing on the beach suffered no casualties from the beach defences.

For this action, he was awarded the Distinguished Service Order.

Lieutenant William Grant Herbert commanded a platoon of "B" Company of the Queen's Own Rifles which was an assault company during the landing at Bernières-sur-Mer at approximately 0800 hours. The company was met with severe machine-gun fire from a pill box 100 yards to its front and within the first few minutes there were sixty-five casualties. Lieutenant Herbert, himself suffering from a head wound and shrapnel in the leg, ran forward with two of his men and assaulted the pill box with grenades and Sten machine carbine. As a result of this act, the pill box was put out of action and the remainder of the company were able to proceed with their all-important task of eliminating the beach defences. Due to this complete disregard for his personal safety and his bravery and determination to carry out his commander's intention, the task was successfully completed and the company which followed in the landing on the beach suffered no casualties from the beach defences.

For this action, he was awarded the Military Cross.

During the assault on the beach at Bernières-sur-Mer at approximately 0800 hours, the company met with very severe machine-gun fire from a pill box 100 yards to its front and there were, within the first few moments, sixty-five casualties. Lance/Corporal René Tessier of the Queen's Own Rifles, along with Lieutenant W.G. Herbert and Rifleman Chicoski, ran forward and assaulted the pill box with grenades and Sten machine carbines. As a result of this act, the pill box was put out of action and the remainder were able to proceed with their all-important task of eliminating the beach defences. Due to this act of gallantry and complete disregard for personal safety, the task was successfully completed and the company which followed in the landing on this beach suffered no casualties from the beach defences.

For this action, he was awarded the Military Medal.

When "B" Company of the Queen's Own Rifles assaulted the beach at Bernières-sur-Mer at approximately 0800 hours, 6 June 44, the company met with very severe machine-gun fire from a pill box 100 yards to its front, and within the first few moments there were sixty-five casualties. Rifleman Chicoski along with Lieutenant Herbert and Lance/Corporal Tessier, ran forward and assaulted the pill box with grenades and Sten machine carbine. As a result of this act, the pill box was put out of action and the remainder of the company was able to proceed with their all-important task of eliminating the beach defences. Due to this act of gallantry and complete disregard for personal safety, the task was completed successfully and the companies which followed in the landing on this beach suffered no casualties from the beach defences. The devotion to duty of Rifleman Chicoski, who so loyally followed the lead of his platoon commander, undoubtedly saved the lives of many of his comrades.

For this action, he was awarded the Military Medal.

Meanwhile, on the beach, *Sapper John Duval of the 16th Canadian Field Company RCE was an operator of an armoured D7 bulldozer who had landed at D plus 60 minutes, pulling a tractor of road-making material. His task was to clear and maintain the route inland from Nan White Beach through Bernières. On being told by an officer that there were no other bulldozers available as yet, he unhooked his trailer and in twenty minutes constructed three wheeled-vehicle exits over the sea wall, making it possible to get the first wheeled vehicles off the beach. This act was done under enemy small arms and severe mortar fire. The next day, Sapper Duval carried out further road clearing tasks under fire.*

For this action, he was awarded the Military Medal.

The supporting field artillery regiments began landing their self-propelled 105-mm guns on Nan White beach shortly after 0900 hours. The 19th Field Artillery Regiment had its first gun in action at 0920 hours.

Gunner Harold Roe Chaplin, a driver with the 99th Field Battery of the 19th Canadian Field Regiment, drove his vehicle from the LCT and was immediately tied up on the beach with it and other vehicles by a heavy traffic jam. All vehicles and personnel came under very heavy mortar, rifle and machine-gun fire It was necessary for everyone, for personal safety, to leave their vehicles and seek shelter against the embankment. Gunner Chaplin was wounded in three places and three self-propelled guns took fire from the bombing.

It became apparent that other equipment might suffer loss by fire if left there. Gunner Chaplin, although thrice wounded, with utter disregard for personal safety, went under this heavy mortar and machine-gun fire and drove his vehicle, as well as others, to the exit on the beach and subsequently to the gun position where the guns were able to be placed in action and put to their correct use. Gunner Chaplin had to be carried from his vehicle as he was unable to move after performing this brave task.

Gunner Chaplin, by his devotion to duty, personal courage and determined work to see the job well done was an inspiration to all and is worthy of commendation for same.

For this action, he was awarded the Military Medal.

Major McGregor Young was Action OC of the 19th Canadian Field Regiment in the assault at Bernières-sur-Mer. He proceeded through the streets on foot with his leading self-propelled guns and, regardless of his own personal safety, indicated many enemy strong points over "open sights". The destruction of these strong points materially influenced the successful passage of men and material through the beach defences. Major Young consistently carried out forward reconnaissance and observer work, remaining in forward and exposed positions to effectively control the fire of his Regiment in initial actions against enemy counter attacks, in spite of efforts to dislodge him. His cool judgment and steadfast courage produced heavy deterrent fire, rendering great service to the infantry he was supporting. His commander considered his conduct both an example and inspiration to all.

For this action, he was awarded the Distinguished Service Order.

On this morning, Captain Leonard Elliot Cowan was in command of a section of the 22nd Canadian Field Ambulance which landed with, and in support of, the Queen's Own Rifles of Canada in the assault on Bernières-sur-Mer. For one and a half hours he directed and treated casualties on the beach under heavy artillery and mortar fire, as well as cross fire from snipers. By his gallantry and leadership, and a complete disregard for his own safety, he kept his section together and cleared many wounded to safety under the sea wall. He continued to serve with his section, although suffering from a ruptured gastric ulcer, and only reported for treatment when casualties in his area were completely cleared. He was operated upon immediately after reporting ill.

For this action, he was awarded the Military Cross.

Riflemen of Regina Rifles Regiment storm ashore in front of the Courseulles strong point.
Credit/David Craig.

Green Beach of Nan Sector

Just after 0800 hours, the two assault companies of the Regina Rifles Regiment touched down on Green Beach to face the eastern half of the Courseulles strong point. The Canadians immediately met strong resistance from the concrete casemates and a line of fortified houses which the preliminary bombardment had not satisfactorily damaged.

On June 6 at Courseulles-sur-Mer, "A" Company was right assaulting company of the 1st Battalion, The Regina Rifle Regiment, touching down at H hour on Nan Green Beach. Sergeant John Alexander Snyder, was commanding a platoon, as the company was one officer under strength. Very heavy machine-gun fire, from buildings on the promenade and a large pill box at the mouth of the river, swept the whole company beach and caused severe casualties.

Sergeant Snyder, seeing that to hesitate would only cause more casualties, led the balance of his platoon across the open beach into protection of the sand dunes. He then proceeded to carry out the task given his platoon by personally leading his men along the edge of the promenade to the buildings where the machine guns were situated and silencing them.

With further acts of gallantry later in Normandy, his many examples of leadership and courage were an inspiration to the men who served under him.

For these actions, he was awarded the Croix de Guerre with Silver Star.

Rifleman Oscar Albert Johnson of the Regina Rifles crawled forward the full length of the beach under heavy enemy machine-gun fire, cutting his way through six feet of wire which was covered by enemy weapons. He then went back and assumed the leadership of the remainder of his section, leading them through the wire and into the enemy slit trenches. From there he continued to move forward as a sniper, well ahead of his company. This move was done entirely on his own initiative and he displayed rare courage and resourcefulness; at no time previously had he ever had charge of a section of men.

For this action, he was awarded the Military Medal.

Rifleman Charles Hamilton Moorehead of the Regina Rifles was a stretcher bearer and was twice wounded while landing. Despite this fact, for at least forty-five minutes while "A" Company was still on the beach, he was seen carrying dead and wounded out of the water to the beach and administering to them. As the tide moved in, he moved them forward again. During all this time, the beach was subjected to heavy light machine-gun fire and mortar fire. When last seen by the Company Commander, he was dragging a wounded soldier out of a depth of approximately three feet of water, struggling and faltering with every step, yet always regaining his feet and lifting the man forward. This soldier was wounded on 6 June and evacuated through the normal medical channels to Hospital.

For this action, he was awarded the Military Medal.

Lance/Sergeant Walter Douglas Armstrong of the Regina Rifles, under heavy machine-gun fire on the beach, crawled forward with a light machine-gun. He located an enemy machine-gun position which was being supported by enemy riflemen from slit trenches and, with the assistance of two riflemen, cleaned out the enemy position. During this time they were under fire from another enemy light machine-gun. It was due to this effort that the remainder of the company was able to move forward and get the buildings on the regiment's right flank. It was afterwards discovered that during this time, Lance/Sergeant Armstrong had been wounded while on the beach, a bullet having passed right through one leg and grazing another. When asked by his Company Commander about his wound, he showed the leg that was not grazed. After taking out a light machine-gun position, he crawled back to his Company under fire, pinpointed another light machine-gun position and then crawled back to support the Company with fire while it did a flanking movement. He remained in command of his men during the remainder of the morning, leading them forward with a light machine-gun and only returned to the beach dressing station when ordered to do so by his Company commander at approximately 1400 hours on 6 June.

For this action, he was awarded the Military Medal.

As on the other beaches, the assault engineers came in with the leading infantry.

Sapper Ralph Charles Spencer, of the 6th Canadian Field Company RCE, landed on Nan Green with "A" Company of the Regina Rifles. As soon as he left the landing craft, he was wounded in the left knee and leg by light machine-gun fire from the beach defences. Notwithstanding his considerable wounds, and with complete disregard for his own safety, Sapper Spencer moved about the beach dragging the wounded further ahead of the rising tide. By this action, which took place under heavy fire, Sapper Spencer, though out of the fighting himself, undoubtedly saved at least six wounded men from death by drowning.

For this action, he was awarded the Military Medal.

As the Regina Riflemen managed to fight their way off the beach, they were then faced with clearing fortified blocks of houses in the village. As they moved away from the beach, the Canadians found the Germans were filtering back into their old positions by means of "tunnels and trenches".

In this situation, *Lieutenant William David Grayson of the Regina Rifles showed high qualities of leadership and bravery on at least three occasions. While entering a block of houses in Courseulles, an enemy light machine-gun crew made a dash with their weapon from the house behind the sea wall towards their slit trenches. Lieutenant Grayson dashed over, armed only with a Colt automatic pistol and forced the surrender of the gun crew, sending them back as prisoners. Later the same morning, he led three men from the safety of a block of houses into a very large pill box from which the company had been subjected to heavy machine-gun fire, cleared it out and captured at least ten prisoners from this tunnel position. On the same day, he led five men to clean up a large tunnel along a river bank from which twenty-five prisoners were taken and numerous others killed. These are only the mere outstanding examples of this officer's bravery and disregard for his own safety throughout the day. He was very highly recommended for an award.*

For this action, he was awarded the Military Cross.

Gunner Jack Holtzman, of the 13th Canadian Field Artillery Regiment, was a signaller assigned to accompany an artillery captain landing on the assault wave as a Forward Fire Observer. After his captain was wounded, he carried on and called forward the tanks of the 2nd Royal Marine Armoured Support

Regiment to knock out an enemy pillbox which had opened up on the rear of the Regina Rifles. He directed fire successfully and neutralized the enemy position, thus enabling the Canadian infantry to engage the enemy frontally with confidence and energy. Gunner Holtzman's actions, under heavy fire and most difficult conditions, played an effective part in the success of the operations.

For this action, he was awarded the Military Medal.

Once off the beaches, each company of the Regina Rifles was to move inland, concentrate in the area of the village of Reviers, and seize the crossing over the River Seulles. All units of the brigade would then move on to capture the high ground further inland as the final objectives of the day.

At approximately 1700 hours, Corporal Garbutt Chapman of the 6th Canadian Field Company RCE, with half a section of Number 2 Platoon, was advancing with "B" Company of the Regina Rifles. South of the village of Reviers, Number 10 Platoon leading was engaged by light machine-gun fire and pinned to the ground. Heavy mortar fire from an opposite hill followed, and Corporal Chapman, from his position at Platoon Headquarters, perceived that these mortar bombs had caused casualties in his section. Disregarding the danger from shrapnel, he at once moved back over very open ground to where his men were lying, and with great coolness rallied them, withdrawing those not wounded to safety. Corporal Chapman displayed further courage in actions on June 8, described in his full citation.

This non-commissioned officer, on both occasions, displayed great initiative, leadership and coolness under fire and had, by these qualities, prevented many casualties.

For this action, he was awarded the Military Medal.

As in the other regiments, the regimental padre was close at hand to provide support to the men under his care. *H/Captain Graham Moffat Jamieson was attached to the Regina Rifle Regiment as their Chaplain, displaying a very high standard of courage and coolness under fire. He landed with "B" Company at H minus 20 minutes and throughout the battle on D-day assisted with the wounded and made arrangements for the dead.*

During the battles over the next ten days, he displayed great courage throughout. He was constantly and tirelessly employed attending to the wounded, and again making arrangements for the dead, both our own and the enemy. His example was an inspiration to all ranks and his courage and thoughtfulness under fire were outstanding.

For this action, he was awarded the Military Cross.

"The Assault: D-Day". Painted by Capt. O. Fisher.
Copyright THE CANADIAN WAR MUSEUM/12469

Red and Green Beaches of Mike Sector

The landing of the Royal Winnipeg Rifles in front of the western half of the Courseulles strong point is described by Colonel C.P. Stacey:

The battalion diary remarked grimly "The bombardment having failed to kill a single German or silence one weapon, ["B" and "D" Companies] had to storm their positions 'cold'— and did so without hesitation." "B" Company met heavy machine-gun, shell and mortar fire beginning when the L.C.A.s were 700 yards from the beach. This continued until touch-down, and as the men leaped from the craft many were hit "while still in the water".[13]

Peter Simonds wrote that the Royal Winnipeg Rifles faced "what were perhaps the strongest beach defences in Normandy - consisting of five large reinforced concrete blockhouses about 30 feet square with numerous machine gun positions between them in concrete strong points amongst the sand dunes . . . Despite the steel and concrete and mines, the Winnipegs broke into the beach defences in the most savage and furious fighting on the whole Normandy front on D-Day."[14]

"B" Company of the Royal Winnipeg Rifles, one platoon of "C" Company, one section of pioneers, plus one and a half sections of No. 6 Field Company, RCE, were under command of Captain Philip Edwin Gower. Eye-witnesses of his command stated that throughout this action and, in spite of having lost his helmet during the landing, Captain Gower stood upright on the beach, coolly directing the employment of his sub-units. By his personal example of bravery, skill and daring, he reduced the defences one by one until the beach defences were overcome. Had it not been for this officer's courage and outstanding devotion to duty in the face of tremendous odds, the landing and advance inland of the remainder of the Battalion would have been seriously hampered. It was considered that this officer's bravery, determination and dauntless leadership contributed tremendously to the Battalion's successful advance to its Brigade objective.

For this action, he was awarded the Military Cross.

Colonel C.P. Stacey later highlighted the fierceness of this struggle: " When the strongpoint was clear, 'B' Company had been reduced to the company commander (Capt. P.E. Gower) and 26 men."[15]

---

13   Stacey, *Victory*, p. 104

14   Peter Simonds, *Maple Leaf Up, Maple Leaf Down*(New York: Island Press Co-operative Inc, 1946), p. 148.

15   Stacey, *Victory*, p. 104

While the reinforced "B" Company touched down on Mike Red, "D" Company of the Royal Winnipeg Rifles landed on Mike Green, further to the west and somewhat clear of the actual strong point area.

Major Lockhart Ross Fulton, commanding "D" Company and one section of pioneers, Royal Winnipeg Rifles, assaulted Green Beach of Mike Sector and captured the objective of Graye-sur-Mer against severe opposition, gapping a minefield in the process. The assault and advance inland was led by Major Fulton with outstanding gallantry, skill and cool daring, his superb qualities of leadership and courage serving as an inspiration to the entire Battalion and contributing largely to the successful advance inland. Further actions by Major Fulton on 8 June against a German counter attack contributed to his award. Major Fulton's personal bravery, his complete disregard for his own safety and his coolness and skill in leading his command are considered to be in keeping with the highest traditions of the service.

Captain Lockhart Ross Fulton, "D" Company of the Royal Winnipeg Rifles, who was awarded the Distinguished Service Order for his actions on landing on Mike Green Beach.
NATIONAL ARCHIVES OF CANADA/PA-131271.

For this action, he was awarded the Distinguished Service Order.

Lieutenant John Mitchell was in command of the leading platoon of "D" Company, the left forward company of the battalion. Small enemy localities were scattered across the axis of advance and fire so heavy that Lieutenant Mitchell was compelled to move in advance of his leading section in order to maintain momentum. Approaching Creully from the left, Lieutenant Mitchell was crossing the River Seulles when he came under terrific cross-fire from two enemy machine-guns on the opposite bank in the woods. This officer managed to cross the river but two men of the leading section were hit, causing the remainder to go to ground. Lieutenant Mitchell was, at this time, wounded in the hand.

Returning to the north bank of the river through a hail of fire, Lieutenant Mitchell managed to summon a troop of the 6th Canadian Armoured Regiment to his aid, gathered his platoon and charged across the bridge against the machine-gun positions.

Lieutenant Mitchell's gallantry, prompt action and cool disregard for his personal safety in neutralizing the enemy position contributed immeasurably toward maintaining the vital impetus of the advance and in gaining the company's portion of the battalion objective. Through this day's action, Lieutenant Mitchell's skill, bravery and coolness in leadership were outstanding.

For this action, he was awarded the Military Cross.

In the struggle on the front of the 7th Brigade, the assaulting infantry had the advantage that the DD tanks of "A" Squadron of the 1st Hussars landed almost simultaneously. The Hussar's regimental history describes their landing:

> Seven DDs succeeded in passing through the hail of shell, mortar and small arms fire that the Germans threw out over the water wherever they could see the odd-looking two feet of canvas screen protruding . . . The sudden appearance of tanks on the beaches in front of their positions had momentarily disorganized the German gunners . . . Landing on the right of 3rd Troop, Capt. Powell's tank was fired upon from a concrete fort. An armour piercing shot hit the 75-mm, went about half way through the barrel and glanced off taking a gouge out of the turret . . . As soon as the anti-tank guns on the beach had been liquidated, the seven DD tanks began to cruise up and down the beach engaging the machine gun nests.[16]

---

16   *Col A. Brandon Conroy, A History of the First Hussars Regiment 1856-1980,* p. 52.

Captain John Wilson Powell was second in command of "A" Squadron, the 6th Canadian Armoured Regiment (1st Hussars). On touching down on Mike Green Beach at approximately 0800 hours, he was immediately engaged by an anti-tank gun in a concrete casemate. Before being able to neutralize the gun, his tank was hit three times, the third shot putting his master gun out of action. Captain Powell moved his tank forward and neutralized the enemy gun with his Browning machine-gun whilst directing the fire of the other tanks onto enemy gun positions.

During this action, he received an injury in his left hand and, while still on the beach, he changed tanks and continued to engage the enemy coast defences, as well as organize part of the squadron which had succeeded in landing on his section of the beach. When the beach exits were cleared, he moved forward and continued to support the infantry until his tank broke a track. He and his crew repaired the track and rejoined his squadron as soon as possible. He then continued to render valuable service and was an example to all ranks by his cool actions.

For this action, he was awarded the Military Cross.

Corporal Henry John Beverley of the 1st Hussars was a crew commander of a special assault tank which landed near Graye-sur-Mer. Because his periscope was clouded he was steering the tank from the deck and, while doing so, was shot through the shoulder. He managed to regain his steering positions and, under heavy fire, safely guided his tank the remaining three hundred yards to the beach, through the beach mine defences.

Although painfully wounded, he directed the fire of his tank and succeeded in knocking out a 75-mm infantry gun in a casemate, two fortified machine-gun nests, and two unfortified machine-gun posts. Thus, he was largely instrumental in enabling the infantry to storm successfully the primary objective. At the completion of the beach assault, he was given a tank in which the master gun had been disabled. He carried on, however, with his machine-guns, supporting the infantry throughout D-Day as far as one mile south of Creully. He remained on duty with the squadron until 1100 hours the next day when he was evacuated.

By his courageous leadership and determination, he was instrumental in getting the infantry onto their objective and saved them countless casualties.

For this action, he was awarded the Military Medal.

Trooper Helgi Stephen Runolfson of the 1st Hussars was the driver of a special assault tank which launched before H hour off the beach of Graye-sur-Mer on Mike Green sector. The tank drowned and the crew took shelter on the rear deck while the enemy brought down heavy mortar and machine-gun fire. The crew commander was wounded and washed overboard. Trooper Runolfson, without regard for his own safety, went after the crew commander and tried to save him, but was unsuccessful due to the rough sea. After two hours in the water, he was able to get ashore. He then picked up a German rifle with ammunition and, although suffering from the effects of immersion, fought his way forward with the leading elements of the infantry until he was able to rejoin his unit.

For this action, he was awarded the Military Medal.

Major William Dudley Brooks of the 1st Hussars commanded a squadron of special assault tanks in the assault on Mike Beach. This equipment had never been used before in operations and was launched under very unfavourable weather conditions. Major Brooks displayed outstanding leadership and inspiration to his squadron and is responsible for having placed a large proportion of his special assault tanks on the beach despite all hazards of weather, beach obstacles and enemy action. He immediately attacked the beach defences with great courage and skill which made it possible for the assault infantry to land on the beach and go forward to gain their objectives. The action and leadership of this officer largely influenced the success of the assault landing and the gaining of the beachhead.

For this action, he was awarded the Distinguished Service Order.

Lieutenant William Patrick Hair of the 12th Field Regiment RCA was acting in the capacity of Regimental survey officer. He landed at Courseulles-sur-Mer at approximately 0815 hours with the unit reconnaissance party immediately after the assaulting companies of the Royal Winnipeg Rifles. Because the beach exits were still blocked by the enemy, it was decided to deploy the guns on the water's edge. This necessitated the reconnaissance and survey being carried out at once under the fire of enemy machine-guns and mortars. Lieutenant Hair set up his instruments on the sand dunes in full view of the enemy and had his survey completed by 0900 hours when the guns arrived. The determination and coolness of Lieutenant Hair during this most important phase of the invasion and in the subsequent positions in the beach-head were important factors in producing the quick and accurate artillery support required by the 7th Canadian Infantry Brigade in the capture and retention of its objective.

For his action, he was awarded the Croix de Guerre with Vermilion Star.

Major Alexander Gibson Goldie of the 12th Field Regiment RCA acted as a Forward Observation Officer for the ship-borne guns of his regiment, directing their fire onto the enemy's beach defences. This necessitated his small craft being in the forefront of the invading fleet to within range of the enemy's small arms weapons. Under very difficult conditions of poor visibility, rough seas, and enemy gun fire, he effectively neutralized their defences thus enabling the 6th Canadian Armoured Regiment and the Royal Winnipeg Rifles to get ashore with comparatively light casualties.

On landing, he assumed the duties of second-in-command and deployed the regiment on the immediate beaches, affording continuous support to the infantry. (Major Goldie distinguished himself in further actions, as detailed in his periodic award.)

For his actions, he was awarded the Distinguished Service Order.

Lance/Sergeant Alexander Semple of the 18th Canadian Field Company RCE landed at H Hour on the beach west of Courseulles. Although working conditions were entirely adverse and unexpected, he assembled his party and cleared a 50-yard gap through obstacles on the beach to permit landing craft to beach unhindered. Working in four feet of water, hampering the troops, and in order to have time, Lance/Sergeant Semple led the men in removing obstacles without checking mines, shells and attached charges for traps. The gap was completed under enemy fire and Lance/Sergeant Semple, although wounded, continued to lead his party until work was completed when he led them to shelter and assisted in taking enemy prisoners and in clearing wounded.

For this action, he was awarded the Military Medal.

Lance/Corporal William Alfred Amos, 18th Field Company RCE, landed with his platoon at H Hour on the beach west of Courseulles and commenced clearing beach obstacles to permit the landing of troops and equipment. The beach was under machine-gun fire and Lance/Corporal Amos received a painful wound on the elbow, partially disabling him. In spite of his injury, Lance/Corporal Amos continued to operate his team until too weak to continue, when he was evacuated. This junior non-commissioned officer displayed great devotion to duty of beach clearing and little regard for his own safety or injury, and set a wonderful example to the troops working with him.

For this action, he was awarded the Military Medal.

Sergeant James Albert Romain of the 18th Canadian Field Company RCE also landed at H hour. On learning that his platoon commander had not arrived, he immediately assumed control over the beach obstacle clearing parties, including two sections from another field company. Owing to the state of tide, the Beach Master would not permit any immediate work. Sergeant Romain, having made a beach reconnaissance, re-organized his men and arranged for immediate work on receiving the clearance from the Beach Master. In the meantime, he organized rescue parties for wounded infantry on the beaches. Under fire and without any means of intercommunication, he organized all details for the work; as a result, the men cleared one 200-yard gap and one 500-yard gap on the beach within an hour of commencing work. Sergeant Romain personally supervised work over one-half mile of beach clearance, the result of which enabled landing craft to enter safely to disembark troops and equipment. Throughout the entire period, he was on the beaches under enemy fire and in considerable personal danger from exploding mines and craft. This non-commissioned officer displayed great initiative, coolness, disregard for personal safety and good powers of leadership.

For this action, he was awarded the Military Medal.

During the assault on Courseulles, Major Henry Archibald Proctor, a medical officer of 3rd Division Headquarters, landed while the beaches were still subjected to intense fire. At great personal risk to himself, he gave first aid to the wounded on the beach. He personally assisted with and directed the collection of casualties under the sea wall such that they were under cover from enemy fire and out of reach of the advancing tide, thereby saving many lives.

Throughout the remainder of the day, he continued to attend the wounded in the beach area in the presence of enemy snipers and bombing attacks without regard to his personal safety. On his own initiative, he made his way into St Aubin-Sur-Mer while it was still occupied by the enemy, and there gave first aid to some seventy-five casualties in the area — all of whom were collected on the following day.

For this action, he was awarded the Distinguished Service Order.

Allied landing craft on the beach, as seen
from a German gun position.
D.I. Grant/NATIONAL ARCHIVES OF CANADA/PA-128792.

The Western Flank of Mike Sector

On the far right of the Canadian landing area, one company of the 1st Battalion, Canadian Scottish Regiment had one of the easier touch-downs. Here, according to one Colonel C.P. Stacey, the Canadian Scottish "reported that it landed with slight opposition, and the platoon which had the job of knocking out the 75-mm casemate north of Vaux approached it 'only to find — thanks to the Royal Navy — the pill-box was no more'"[17]. Even so, Red Beach was still a dangerous place:

At approximately 0830 hours, while making the run-in to Mike Red Beach from the HMCS Prince Henry, in LCA "5" (1103), the coxswain was killed outright. Corporal Charles Franklin Mowatt of the 14th Canadian Field Ambulance took over the controls and landed the LCA while under severe mortar and machine-gun fire. Then, on landing, he organized his sub-section of eight men and immediately attended casualties on the beach while under fire until he finally made contact with his officer, Captain A.B. Murphy. He continued his duties on the beach until the complete section left. He also carried on throughout the whole day of the action with the 1 Canadian Scottish.

For this action, he was awarded the Military Medal.

"C" Company's platoons quickly got off the beach, with Lieutenant V.R. Scheldrup's Number 13 Platoon moving up the centre on the road to Vaux. They quickly encountered resistance and had to fight their way through machine-gun posts which had not been touched by the bombardment. As they approached the village of Ste Croix, it became apparent that they had hit the heart of a well-concealed German defensive position. These positions were eventually overcome with the assistance of artillery and some tanks from the 1st Hussars.

For the rest of the day, they continued an aggressive advance, destroying further machine-gun and mortar positions until they reached their final objective six miles inland. In this advance, as described by Reginald Roy, "no platoon had been hit harder than Lieutenant Scheldrup's. He had come

---

17   Stacey, *Victory*, p. 104

ashore with 45 men under his command. At the end of the day when he, himself, was ordered back to have his wounds dressed, there were only 19 men left."[18]

In the assault and advance to the hinterland, Lieutenant Vilhelm Roger Schjelderup's outstanding leadership and courage was a decided inspiration to his men when he and his platoon of the 1st Battalion, Canadian Scottish Regiment attacked at least four enemy machine-gun positions in areas Vaux and Ste Croix-sur-Mer. Despite a wound received in this action, he carried on until the night of D-Day and left only when his platoon was safely dug in its position for the night.

For this action, he was awarded the Military Cross.

---

18   Reginald Roy, *Ready for the Fray,* (Vancouver: Evergreen Press, 1958) p. 227.

.

THE 6TH OF JUNE —
THE ADVANCE INLAND

Moving Out of Bernières

By midday, the 7th and 8th Brigades had broken through the German beach defences and were pushing inland, and the reserve brigade, the 9th, had landed. There were, however, scattered pockets of resistance and one of the most troublesome was outside Bernières. Here a German anti-tank gun blocked the exit.

Lieutenant Walter Moisan, commanding a platoon of Le Régiment de la Chaudière, was ordered to advance from an assembly area in Bernières to capture an 88-mm gun battery position protected by a series of trenches and machine-gun emplacements and an anti-tank gun covering the approaches from the beachhead. The presence of this gun made it impossible for our tanks supporting the company to give adequate fire support to the infantry. Lieutenant Moisan commanded the leading platoon and, despite lack of tank support, he led his platoon to the gun position fifteen hundred yards inland. A few hundred yards from the gun position, his forward section was pinned down by small arms fire from the trenches. This officer worked his way forward to his leading section and led them to a position some thirty yards from the gun, from where the gun was put out of action. An explosion took place in the enemy position and Lieutenant Moisan's clothing was set afire. Although seriously burned, this officer urged his men forward and his platoon succeeded in capturing the enemy position. Throughout this action he displayed great devotion to duty and his personal courage was an inspiration to his men.

For this action, he was awarded the Military Cross.

Corporal Bruno Vennes of Le Régiment de la Chaudière was in command of the leading section of the leading company in the advance of the Battalion from the beaches inland. He came under fire from the 88-mm gun position which was to be captured by his company. After his platoon commander was

German Anti-Tank Gunner. Painted by Capt. O. Fisher.
Copyright THE CANADIAN WAR MUSEUM/12507.

wounded, he moved his section to an assault distance from the gun and, in spite of machine-gun fire, he advanced into the position, using hand grenades to capture the objective. The actual cleaning up of the gun position was his own individual work. As soon as the gun was captured, he reorganized his section and proceeded to mop up the infantry position. Throughout the whole action, Corporal Vennes' loyalty to his platoon commander and his coolness under fire were an example which urged his men forward.

For this action, he was awarded the Military Medal.

Captain Tom Bond, of the 19th Canadian Field Artillery Regiment RCA, by his personal courage, determination and utter disregard for personal danger and devotion to duty, was responsible for the successful advance of Le Régiment de la Chaudière, to which he was attached as a Forward Observation Officer. Captain Bond, throughout the Chaudière's advance from the beaches, stood forward with the leading company in order to give good support to the infantry. On two occasions, although under heavy enemy artillery and mortar fire, he remained in his Observation Post until the capture of the objective. In one particular instance, in the vicinity of Le Hamel, he was shelled out of his Observation Post and, while keeping fire going on his objective, he went forward to another Observation Post, still under heavy fire, to continue giving valuable support to the infantry. Throughout the operation, Captain Bond's coolness and confidence under fire was observed to be an inspiration to all.

For this action, he was awarded the Military Cross.

Assault on the Tailleville Position

Reginald Roy described the advance from St Aubin inland:
The North Shore Regiment had fought steadily from St Aubin to Tailleville, but the latter village, containing the Headquarters of the 2nd Battalion, 736th Grenadier Regiment, was proving to be a hard nut to crack. Here the enemy was well dug in, with numerous tunnels running from one gun pit to another, and its weapons were sited so as to cover all approaches. [1]

Major Ralph Herman Daughney commanded "C" Company of the North Shore Regiment. *This Company landed as a reserve company and had, as its objective, the penetration task of seizing the Coastal Artillery Headquarters at Tailleville. The garrison of this place had developed the defence system well with the result that, when first attacked, the defence proved very elastic. Major Daughney immediately reorganized his Company after the first assault and, after hard fighting, eventually completely disposed of all resistance with the assistance of two troops of tanks of the 10th Canadian Armoured Regiment. Throughout this action, the unflinching decisiveness and personal disregard of danger inspired his junior officers and men into performing an excellent job on this, their first action under fire. This permitted the Battalion to advance inland quickly and eliminate a number of observation points and various weapons which were firing on the beach area.*

For this action, he was awarded the Distinguished Service Order.

---

1   Reginald Roy, *1944 The Canadians in Normandy* (Toronto: Macmillan of Canada, 1984) p. 22.

Private Charles Herbert Butland was in "C" Company during the North Shore Regiment's attack against the enemy positions at Tailleville. Enemy in dug-in positions held up the advance to the objective of Private Butland's section. There was no way in which fire could be brought to bear on the enemy from cover. Recognizing this fact and the seriousness of this hold-up, Private Butland stepped into the open and advanced firing his light machine-gun from the hip, directly into the enemy, effectively silencing their fire. During this action, he was under such intense fire from this and at least one other position, that his web equipment was actually cut off his shoulders by the enemy fire. By his quick action, the section was enabled to advance after only a brief pause.

The following day, Private Butland was wounded in the neck by shrapnel. He had his wound dressed and at once returned to his section and continued to display a great daring in the use of this light machine-gun. During all the operations of his section on the first two days of action, Private Butland's skill with his weapon was directly responsible for the success of their attacks and his personal disregard for danger inspired a high degree of confidence in all his section.

For this action, he was awarded the Military Medal.

Tailleville was partially surrounded by a high wall, making it even more difficult to come to grips with the defenders. A hole was found in the north-east corner of the wall and some of the North Shores managed to slip through this hole. Lieutenant G.M. Fawcett led his men through to reach the west end of the village, while Company mortars helped keep the enemy's heads down.[2]

Lieutenant George Malcolm Fawcett of the North Shore Regiment showed remarkable steadiness and leadership throughout two days of difficult fighting. On June 6th, he rallied his platoon on the beach under fire, working them off the beach and seized his initial objective exactly on time according to plan. Later during the assault on Tailleville on D-Day, Lieutenant Fawcett personally led his platoon in to breach the town wall and was the first to gain a foothold

---

2   Will Bird, *North Shore (New Brunswick) Regiment* (Brunswick Press, 1963), p.219.

inside the walled area. Here he at once organized his platoon to clear the area of enemy.

On the 7th of June, this officer showed the same cool courage in leading his platoon against the Radar Station. He fought his way to within 300 yards of the entrance to the Radar Station and held his ground despite heavy enemy mortar fire until he was wounded.

Lieutenant Fawcett remained cool, unhurried and decisive throughout the first two confused days of fighting. This steadiness and courage made itself felt throughout the whole Company.

For this action, he was awarded the Military Cross.

In the attack on Tailleville, the North Shore Regiment gave a detachment of tanks from "C" Squadron of the Fort Garry Horse a great deal of credit for the successful outcome[3]. Captain A.S. Christian of the Fort Garry Horse played a key roll, sending some of his tanks to either side of the strong point in an encircling movement that cut off the German defender's route of retreat. He remained in action despite a bullet wound in his finger and another grazing wound in his head.

In the early afternoon of June 6, Captain Alexander Sutherland Christian of the Fort Garry Horse was in command of a detachment of tanks supporting the infantry of the North Shore Regiment clearing Tailleville. Though wounded in the early part of the attack, he commanded with skill and courage during this successful action. Many enemy were slain and approximately one hundred captured in this strongly defended area. His tank group performed outstanding service in helping forward the North Shore Regiment onto their objective. This greatly assisted the whole advance inland on D-Day. Captain Christian displayed outstanding leadership, personal courage and fortitude.

For this action, he was awarded the Military Cross.

---

3   Vanguard, *The Fort Garry Horse in the Second World War* (Holland, 1945), p.133.

"German defenders surrender at Tailleville".
CREDIT/Davaid Craig.

Private George Stanley Clark of the North Shore Regiment was a member of a section of "A" Company which landed at St Aubin at H plus 5 minutes. Both the section leader and the second-in-command became casualties and Private Clark, on his own initiative, took over command of the section.

In the afternoon, in the vicinity of Tailleville, Private Clark's unit was the forward section of the leading platoon which came under heavy machine-gun and mortar fire. There was no cover for his men near at hand and, recognizing this fact, he unhesitatingly led his men across eight hundred yards of open country under fire to attack the enemy position in the wood and neutralize the fire. By this action, he made it possible for the remainder of "A" Company and the whole of "D" Company to cross the same ground to close with the enemy and carry on with the attack.

During the whole of the operation on D-Day, Private Clark showed himself ready to assume unexpected responsibilities, quick at appreciating difficult situations, and decisive in his action to overcome them. His display of personal courage enabled him to maintain firm control of his men and was at all times an inspiration to all ranks. There is no doubt that his qualities of leadership and resolution made possible this local success of "A" and "D" Companies and thereby contributed greatly to the success of this operation.

For this action, he was awarded the Military Medal.

Canadian troops and traffic congestion on the outskirts of St Aubin-sur-Mer.
Frank L. Dubervill/NATIONAL ARCHIVES OF CANADA/PA-128789.

Civilians of Thaon wave tankmen on their way as they dash inland.
Frank L. Dubervill/NATIONAL ARCHIVES OF CANADA/DND 35384.

The Advance to Colomby-sur Thaon/Anguerny

While the North Shore Regiment was dealing with the stubborn resistance at Tailleville, other elements of the 8th Brigade pushed on toward their intermediate objectives. On the eastern flank, these included the high ground near the villages of Colomby-sur-Thaon, Anisy and Anguerny.

Major Joseph Georges Sevigny commanded "C" Company of Le Régiment de la Chaudière which was acting as the regiment's advance guard during its advance through the villages of Beny-sur-Mer, Basly and Colomby-sur-Thaon to the final objective. This was reached late in the evening of D-Day. During this advance of approximately 4000 metres against villages which were strongly defended by infantry and infantry weapons, the Company was constantly under fire.

Major Sevigny was well forward with his leading troops throughout, and led and directed the efforts of his Company in such a manner that not only were the villages captured but, by his good tactics and aggressive action, he greatly assisted his battalion commander to gain his final objective with a minimum of delay. Major Sevigny showed himself to be brave, resourceful, and possessed of sound judgment. He was an outstanding example to his men, during this their first time in action, in which he displayed personal courage. By his bold actions he contributed greatly to the success of his battalion in gaining its objective and holding it during the first night.

For this action, he was awarded the Distinguished Service Order.

The reserve brigade, the 9th, landing at Bernières, found itself caught up in a massive traffic jam on the congested beaches. It cleared itself from this late in the afternoon and set out riding on tanks or carriers in a dash for the final objectives. Detachments from the division's medium machine-gun battalion, the Cameron Highlanders of Ottawa, accompanied the vanguard.

Lieutenant James Crawford Woodward of the Cameron Highlanders of Ottawa commanded Number 6 Platoon of "B" Company. Just south of Bernières, he single-handedly rushed a small body of enemy who were obstructing the advance of his platoon. Later the same morning, Lieutenant Woodward moved up to the head of the brigade advance and, with no regard for personal safety, got positions for his guns to cover the infantry to move forward. At the village of Busly, he was the first man after the tanks to enter the village. He drove through with determination to see his Brigade commander's intention carried out. He pushed ahead alone at Anguerny, up onto the high ground, to do his reconnaissance so he could get his guns in quickly in case of counter attack. He completed his reconnaissance and brought his platoon into action despite being fired at continually by snipers and being under enemy machine-gun and mortar fire. Lieutenant Woodward, by his example, leadership and drive, was instrumental in speeding up the advance of 8th Canadian Infantry Brigade to its objective.

For this action, he was awarded the Military Cross.

Advance on the Right Flank

The Canadian Scottish, on the right flank of the beachhead, reached their intermediate objective at about 1630 hours. Here they paused only briefly before pushing on deeper, suffering more casualties from enemy mortar and machine-gun positions that had not been touched by the shore bombardment. By dusk, they were six miles inland from the sea. Reginald Roy has written that of all the infantry battalions of the 2nd British Army landing, the Canadian Scottish in its present positions had gone farthest through the enemy's defences ... During this march, Captain W.H.V. Matthews organized a party of men to search barns and buildings en route, flushing out a large number of German stragglers and others, and making the route safer for those coming behind.[4]

On June 6, throughout the assault landing and the advance into the hinterland, Captain William Harold Victor Matthews' conduct was an inspiring example to the men of his Company. On two occasions, when the advance was held up, he led parties of men to clean up centres of resistance, under intense machine-gun and mortar fire on both occasions. [His citation describes further examples of courage under fire on June 8.]

4   Reginald Roy, *Ready for the Fray: The History of the Canadian Scottish Regiment* (Vancouver: Evergreen Press, 1958), p. 226.

His advice, coolness, disregard for personal safety and inspiring leadership saved the situation on many occasions, won praise from all ranks, and were a deciding factor throughout the assault.

For this action, he was awarded the Military Cross.

H/Captain Robert Louden Seaborn, Padre of the 1st Battalion Canadian Scottish Regiment, landed with his unit. He was slightly wounded in the landing craft just prior to landing, but refused to allow himself to be evacuated. As soon as he landed, he began to assist the Medical Officer to attend to the wounded on the beach and on the advance inland. He paid particular attention to nesting the wounded and ensured that their locations were clearly marked. Whenever the battalion stopped to reorganize, after all the wounded were attended to, he began to bury the dead, sometimes moving well out under enemy fire to recover bodies. Difficult as his task was, handicapped by fatigue and lack of transport and equipment, H/Captain Robert Louden Seaborn carried on, not only caring for the wounded, but frequently visiting all ranks in the battalion, giving encouragement with a cheery word and a smile, never thinking of himself but always of the welfare of the men. He is a true Christian and is admired by the whole battalion down to the last man for his fortitude and gallantry.

For these actions, he was awarded the Croix de Guerre with Vermillion Star.

The Beachhead Consolidated

At 2115 hours, General Keller, commanding the 3rd Canadian Infantry Division, sent out his orders for the night. The brigades would hold the ground they had reached, carry out active patrolling and be prepared to meet any German counter-attack the next morning. In the meantime, engineers continued their work on the beaches to clear the obstacles, sunken landing craft, minefields and debris. Constant boat traffic was going on, as supplies poured ashore to support the coming battles for the beachhead. In this narrow foothold that the Allies had secured on the coast, even the beach remained an area of danger.

Sapper Raymond Donald Foster of the 16th Canadian Field Company RCE, was a Despatch Rider during D-Day, requiring him to maintain contact with the Engineer Reconnaissance Officer with the leading infantry and the platoon

Carriers Come Ashore From Landing Craft.
Painting by Capt O. Fisher. Copyright THE CANADIAN WAR MUSEUM/12440.

DRY UNLOADING. Equipment pours ashore from LCTs on Mike Beach, still under fire.
Painting by Capt. O. Fisher. Copyright THE CANADIAN WAR MUSEUM, 12480.

Constructing A Road From the Beach. 3rd Division Beach Party laying a tempory
road at Courseulles-sur-Mer for the movement of heavy transport inland.
Painting by Capt. O. Fisher. Copyright THE CANADIAN WAR MUSEUM/12460.

*commander following immediately behind doing mine clearance of the road.
During the whole of D-Day, he made repeated trips along the road between
Bernières-sur-Mer and Le Mare, regardless of enemy snipers and mortar fire
and, on more than one occasion, travelling when the infantry along the road
were pinned down.*

For this action, he was awarded the Military Medal.

*Sergeant James Edwin Aris, part of 3rd Division's 3rd Tps Company, Royal
Canadian Army Service Corps landed at Bernières at 1400 hours in charge
of ammunition for the Assault Beaching. Disregarding the heavy sniping that
was taking place, he immediately organized his men and supervised the
off-loading of the LCTs and establishment of the Ammunition dump which,
due to his efforts, was carried out efficiently and without casualty. During
the night of 6/7 June, the beach and ammunition dump was heavily bombed,
starting many fires, but the off-loading continued in spite of the illumination
and being under observation from snipers. Throughout this trying period,
through his coolness and determination and devotion to duty, Sergeant Aris*

was an inspiration to his men and successfully accomplished a difficult situation that otherwise might have been chaotic.

Realizing the danger from the air by the illumination from the burning ammunition to all troops and vital equipment on the beach, he organized a party of pioneer troops and attacked the fires which were eventually extinguished. (Sergeant Aris further distinguished himself in later actions in North West Europe, detailed in his recommendation for a periodic award.)

For this action, he was awarded the Military Medal.

COMMANDERS RECEIVING AWARDS

Major General R.F.L. Keller, General Officer Commanding the 3rd Canadian Infantry Division for the landing on Juno Beach, being appointed Commander, Order of the British Empire, by King George VI in a ceremony in Normandy.
NATIONAL ARCHIVES OF CANADA/PA-191064.

Several of the senior commanders of the units participating in the assault were recognized for their leadership.

The most significant recognition occurred a few weeks after the landing, as described by Ross Munro:

King George VI came to Normandy. He visited several formations and at General Montgomery's tactical H.Q. at Creully he held the most unusual investiture of this war. On the lawn of a château where the Army Group Commander had his caravan, the King made General Keller

[General Officer Commanding the 3rd Canadian Infantry Division] a Commander of the Order of the British Empire and also decorated a number of British Officers and men for gallantry.

The ceremony was utterly simple, without red carpets and bands. The King, wearing his naval uniform, stood there in the open, while special Spitfire patrols droned overhead, and honoured these men.

For General Keller, the award of the CBE was a tribute to his work in preparing his 3rd Division for the assault and in carrying out the invasion experiments in the long months of training.[1]

Major-General Rodney Frederick Leopold Keller has proved himself an excellent Staff Officer and also Commander in a succession of appointments. He has commanded the 3rd Canadian Infantry Division since September 1942. He has conducted most ably the training of the several forces which have been under his command and has shown great determination and drive.

During the past nine months, Major-General Keller has been charged with the preparation for battle of a complete assault force, including, and considerably greater than, the 3rd Canadian Infantry Division. He has discharged these responsibilities with marked success.

For these actions, he was appointed a Commander of the Order of the British Empire (CBE).

Major-General Rodney Frederick Leopold Keller, CBE, commanded the 3rd Canadian Infantry Division on D-Day when it landed on the Normandy coast as an assault formation and remained in command throughout the campaign until wounded early in August.

Under this Officer's very capable leadership, the landings on D-Day were forcefully executed and skilfully exploited by his Division. In the weeks that followed the record of this Division in the defence and extension of the

---

1   Terry Copp and Robert Vogel, *Maple Leaf Route: Caen*(Alma, Ontario: Maple Leaf Route, 1983) p. 20.

bridgehead against the most determined opposition was outstanding and it also played an important part in the breakthrough. This officer, through his tactical ability, aggressiveness, sound planning and determination, made a real contribution to the successful outcome of the battle of Normandy.

For these actions, he was appointed an Officer of the Legion of Honour.

The commanders of the two assault brigades also received awards. Terry Copp and Robert Vogel have described them as "men in their thirties, RMC graduates but non-permanent militia men before the war. They had gone through the mill of staff college in Britain and their promotions were evidence of their success . . ."[2]

Brigadier H.W. Foster commanded the 7th Canadian Infantry Brigade, whose leading battalions landed on the western sectors of the Division's zone — Nan Green, and Mike Green and Red Beaches.

Brigadier Harry Wickwire Foster's part in the planning, training for, and execution of the assault landings in Normandy was noteworthy for its achievements. After the initial stages of the operation, his Brigade was continually and savagely counter attacked; it lost over 1200 men in the first few days but never gave up any ground; on the contrary, 7 Canadian Infantry Brigade under Brigadier Harry Wickwire Foster's inspired leadership held steadfastly and inflicted severe casualties upon the Germans, forcing them to withdraw. (Brigadier Foster further distinguished himself in actions following D-Day, detailed in his recommendation for an immediate award).

Throughout all these and subsequent operations, Brigadier Harry Wickwire Foster's quiet determination, confidence and coolness under fire were an inspiration to his commanders and men. His example and devotion to duty have had a very marked influence to his Brigade's successful operations which bear the hallmark of a courageous and determined commander. Brigadier Harry Wickwire Foster's conduct throughout is in accord with the best traditions of the Canadian Army.

For these actions, he was awarded the Distinguished Service Order.

---

2   Copp and Vogel, p. 21.

Brigadier K.G. Blackader commanded the 8th Canadian Infantry Brigade, whose leading battalions landed on the eastern sectors of the Division's zone — Nan White and Red Beaches.

Brigadier Kenneth Gault Blackader, commanding the 8th Canadian Infantry Brigade, landed on the coast of France with the leading troops to execute personally the Infantry Division plan he had prepared. Throughout the day, Brigadier Blackader lent a great encouragement to all his commanders and troops by his presence and great determination to reach the objective set to his troops. By the end of D-Day, the 8th Canadian Infantry Brigade had reached its objective; the capture of ground vital to the corps plan. Throughout the initial and subsequent phases, Brigadier Blackader ceaselessly and tirelessly fought his brigade with skill and great determination. Without regard to person, he visited all his units and by his word and deed was an inspiration to his command. Brigadier Blackader's example is worthy of the best traditions of the Army.

For this action, he was awarded the Distinguished Service Order.

The Regina Rifles, under Lieutenant-Colonel Foster Martin Matheson, carried out the initial assault on 6 June. They reached the Brigade objective on 7 June and, from that time onwards until 11 June, fought off many counter attacks. The fighting spirit, tenacity and high morale of this unit was ascribed to the cool headed and spiriting leadership of Lieutenant-Colonel Matheson. (Lieutenant-Colonel Matheson further distinguished himself in actions following D-Day, detailed in his recommendation for an immediate award.)

For these actions, he was awarded the Distinguished Service Order.

On 6 June 1944, as Commanding Officer of the North Shore Regiment, Lieutenant-Colonel Donald Bowie Buell landed immediately behind his leading companies at St Aubin-sur-Mer and continued to direct his battalion from among the forward troops during its advance inland. As the left assault battalion of the Brigade, the North Shore Regiment had an exposed flank and, in view of the fact that the battalion was also forming a firm base for the operations of a Commando, its progress inland was slower than the remainder of the Brigade, which was advancing on its main axis.

Right from the time of the landing, opposition at all stages was greater than expected and, in carrying out his tasks, the widespread action of his unit made the work of Lieutenant-Colonel Buell all the more difficult. In spite of this, the battalion successively captured each position until its advance was halted by the enemy position at the Radar Station. The battalion was later ordered to by-pass this opposition and carry on to its final objective.

Throughout, Lieutenant-Colonel Buell was well forward with the leading companies, directing and controlling the widespread operations. In doing this, he was forced to make his own decisions as communications with Brigade were frequently broken, but he pressed on and showed great determination to carry out his Commander's intention, thereby contributing greatly to the success of the operation. At no time did he spare himself in the performance of his duty and he was an outstanding example to all ranks.

For these actions, he was awarded the Distinguished Service Order.

On 6 June 1944, as Commanding Officer of the Queen's Own Rifles of Canada, which was one of the assault battalions, Lieutenant-Colonel John Godfrey Spragge landed immediately behind his leading companies at Bernières-sur-Mer and continued to direct his battalion from among the forward troops during the advance inland until the capture of the Brigade's final objective in the evening of D-Day. He then reorganized his battalion on its objective and co-ordinated the defence of his own and the battalion on his right.

After the initial assault, progress was slow and the Queen's Own Rifles of Canada was ordered to push on with all haste in order to ensure that the high ground, which was the final objective, was secured before dark. That this operation was successfully carried out was largely due to the personal drive of this officer. (Lieutenant-Colonel Spragge further distinguished himself in actions following D-Day, detailed in his recommendation for an immediate award.)

For these actions, he was awarded the Distinguished Service Order.

Major (Acting Lieutenant-Colonel) Franklyn Everhart White of the 6th Canadian Armoured Regiment (1st Hussars) was considerably responsible for the success of his regiment in the assault on France due to his untiring efforts prior to the invasion. The regiment was assaulting with DD tanks, a new and hazardous type of weapon. Without regard to his own personal safety, he carried out experiments with these tanks which subsequently decreased their risk and undoubtedly saved the lives of many who used them.

When he landed at Bernières-sur-Mer, no exits had been completed and the beach was under heavy enemy mortar and machine-gun fire, and traffic was piling up. He got out of his tank and walked calmly up and down the beach, endeavouring to find an exit. His example of complete coolness at that critical time was an inspiration to the officers and men of the regiment. (Major White further distinguished himself in actions following D-Day, detailed in his recommendation for a periodic award.)

For these actions, he was awarded the Distinguished Service Order.

Lieutenant-Colonel Ronald Edward Alfred Morton commanded the 10th Canadian Armoured Regiment (Fort Garry Horse). On D-Day and during every action since then in which his regiment had been involved, Lt-Col Morton has shown outstanding leadership, ability and courage in handling his regiment and in the co-operative way he was worked with other arms. It was his skill and determination on D-Day that largely contributed to the successful supporting of the 8th Canadian Infantry Brigade onto their objective which was considered of such importance to the successful landing and subsequent operation of the 3rd Canadian Infantry Division. During this action he personally attacked and destroyed with his tank an enemy battalion headquarters. (Lieutenant-Colonel Morton further distinguished himself in actions following D-Day, as detailed in his recommendation for a periodic award.)

For these actions, he was awarded the Distinguished Service Order.

During all stages of the assault and the days immediately following, Lieutenant-Colonel Lewis Gordon Clarke's 19th Canadian Field Artillery Regiment RCA was in support of the advance of the North Shore Regiment. His steady, cheerful manner under fire and his sound advice and ready efficient co-operation were assets beyond value to all under his command

and to those of the infantry whom he was supporting, and with whom he came into contact. On one occasion, due to his quick thinking, he used his OP tank to enable the infantry to bring back to cover Major V.C. Hamilton, 16th Canadian Field Company RCE who had been wounded by snipers. This he did by interposing his OP tank between Major Hamilton and the snipers, thus saving further casualties. His quick and efficient application of fire without consideration of personal risk was a very material factor in the successes obtained.

For these actions, he was awarded the Order of the British Empire.

Captain V.S. Godfrey, Royal Canadian Navy, Commanding Officer of the Landing Ship, Infantry (LSI) HMCS *Prince Henry* and Senior Officer of the LSIs the Assault Force J-1, received a Mention in Despatches for "*good service in the invasion of Normandy*".

EXTRAORDINARY AWARDS

Flight Lieutenant Maxwell William McClellan of RCAF Overseas Head-quarters was a public relations officer selected to proceed with the D-Day beach parties and, together with another public relations officer, carried out advance news coverage of the Royal Canadian Air Force operations from dawn of D-Day until six days later, when additional public relations staff arrived to assist him. During these days, he was constantly under fire from the ground and the air and largely independent in obtaining food, shelter and transportation. The earliest first-hand pictures featuring Royal Canadian Air Force operations over Normandy, including the opening of the first "strip", were obtained through the determination of this officer. He has continued to serve on the Normandy front since the day of his arrival. The courage, disregard of personal danger and determination displayed by this officer under enemy fire are most praiseworthy.

For his actions, he was appointed a Member of the Order of the British Empire.

Flight Lieutenant Errol Quarrier Semple, RCAF, was decorated for his leadership of a group of air force personnel who had been shot down in enemy territory and were evading capture. Flying as a second pilot aboard a 233 Squadron Dakota aircraft on a D-Day supply dropping mission, he and his crew companions were forced to crash-land after their aircraft had been extensively damaged and set on fire by anti-aircraft fire. They landed near the city of Caen in a field full of anti-glider obstacles. Flight Lieutenant Semple suffered a deep head wound that bled profusely until tightly bound. The others were badly shaken up and one had damage to his ribs.

The evaders split up into two groups and moved south to an abandoned house on the edge of the village of Giberville, where friendly French civilians gave them food, shelter and civilian clothing. They later moved to the nearby village of Tilly la Campagne and remained undetected for three weeks despite considerable German activity in the village.

Upon learning that British troops had advanced to a location nearby, Flight Lieutenant Semple split the group into two sections and gave instructions as to how the groups would move to attempt to reach the British lines. While passing through a woods at 0400 hours, they were fired on and lost touch with the second party. At dawn, they crossed 200 yards of open country and stumbled upon a minefield. However, they were recognized by sentries of the British 51st Division and were brought safely into the British lines.

For these actions, Flight Lieutenant Semple was appointed a Member of the Order of the British Empire.

THE FINAL ACTION

At the close of D-Day, the land forces had successfully gained their foothold on the continent. They knew there would be many days of battle ahead before this beach-head could be considered secure. And one of the prime fears of the Supreme Headquarters was to ensure that the flow of men and material would continue to pass across the English Channel fast enough to maintain superiority over the German forces.

The German offensive naval forces in Cherbourg and Le Havre, on the flanks of the Allied crossing route, posed a serious potential threat. The Allied motor torpedo boat (MTB) units therefore became the first line of defence against any possible move by these enemy forces.

The 29th Canadian MTB Flotilla's task was to assist in protecting the eastern flank of the British Assault Area and to attack enemy shipping in the area of Le Havre. Part of the Flotilla moved out late on June 5 to protect the minesweepers from attacks by German motor torpedo boats. The remainder, under Lieutenant-Commander "Tony" Law, cast off at 1400 hours on June 6 and, at some point in mid-Channel, described the scene that met him:

> In the distance the silhouettes of homeward-bound vessels gradually came into clear sight. These were the ships which had carried shock troops for the initial landing on the now blood-stained beaches of Normandy. They were returning to England, some looking naked without their landing craft. Among them were the three Princes, *Prince David*, *Prince Henry*, and *Prince Robert*, all famous Canadian ships which had already survived the invasion of Italy. We signalled "Well done!" Green maple leaves on their funnels were ever-present reminders of home.[1]

---

1   C. Anthony Law, *White Plumes Astern: The Short, Daring Life of Canada's MTB Flotilla* (Halifax: Nimbus Publishing Ltd, 1989), p. 69.

Upon reaching the Assault Fleet off the invasion beaches, the 29th MTB Flotilla received its orders. They were to carry out a night patrol in the area 12 to 14 miles off Cap Le Havre, backed up by destroyer patrols. As daylight slowly vanished, the section of four Canadian MTBs under Lieutenant-Commander Law set off into the howling wind towards their allotted station.

Night Battle Against Six German R-Boats Off Le Havre, France.
Copyright C. Anthony Law/NATIONAL ARCHIVES OF CANADA/C-127038.

The night passed uneventfully, until at about 0200 hours they came upon a battle between a British MTB unit and six strong German R-boats (motor minesweepers). Hal Lawrence has described the action:

> Law spotted six silhouettes, which his radar set confirmed; they were R-boats. At 700 yards, Law's division closed the range and opened fire at 150 yards; Law's boat was hit several times. One hand on the pom-pom, although seriously wounded, continued to feed his gun. In [another MTB], two gunners had also been wounded. All four boats suffered damage or casualties but one R-boat was blown up and another set on fire.[2]

---

2   Hal Lawrence, *Victory At Sea: Tales of His Majesty's Coastal Forces (Toronto: McCelland & Stewart, 1989)*, p. 267.

This action was the start of a long period of small craft battles in the English Channel. For the next two months, the fighting in the Channel became constant and vicious, testing the endurance of the Canadians. As a result, the following officers of the 29th Canadian Motor Torpedo Boat Flotilla received awards for their actions:

Lt-Cmdr Charles Anthony Law — the Distinguished Service Cross;

Lieutenant Craig Bishop — the Distinguished Service Cross;

Lieutenant Charles Arthur Burk — Second Bar to the Distinguished Service Cross;

Lieutenant Donald Chaffey — Mention in Despatches.

For gallantry, skill and determination and undaunted devotion to duty during the landing of Allied Forces on the coast of Normandy.

THE END OF D-DAY

Following the securing of the beachhead, Correspondent Ross Monro came back to the beaches to review the scene of D-Day:

> Those were sombre hours I spent walking through the dunes, the trenches and the casemates where the Canadians had wrought this incredible victory. The German dead were littered over the dunes, by the gun positions. By them, lay Canadians in blood-stained battle-dress, in the sand and in the grass, on the wire and by the concrete of forts. I saw friends I had known, men who had joined the army in the first months of the war, who had trained hard, had endured the tedium of endless manoeuvres and now had died in their first action here on the Norman beach . . .
>
> The wind was blowing hard and the rain fell on this grey beach scene. I drove silently back to the old German headquarters, stirred as I never had been, by the raw, inhuman savage sights of war which that tour of the beach had given me.
>
> "How did they do it?" The question hammered on my mind and the only answer was the indomitable spirit of those magnificent troops.
>
> It was their first fight, and they went into the face of those guns; they clambered and battled over and through the casemates and the trenches; they fought on and on, ferociously, savagely, grimly in the wild tumult that raged that D-Day morning until they had broken through.
>
> The splendid, shining heroism of the Canadian assault troops themselves was the immediate reason for the success of the coastal attack at Courseulles, Bernières and St-Aubin.[1]

---

1 Ross Munro, *Gauntlet to Overlord* (Toronto: The Macmillan Company of Canada, 1945), p. 94.

On the 6th of June, 1944, 359 Canadians died participating in the landing on Juno Beach and the advance inland. Many of these men certainly carried out acts worthy of a gallantry award — such as Corporal J. Klos of the Royal Winnipeg Rifles who, badly shot in the stomach and legs while leaving the assault boat, made his way forward to an enemy machine gun nest. He managed to kill two Nazis before he was mortally felled.[2] Unfortunately, the gallantry awards could not be awarded posthumously to such men.

There were others, like Lieutenant J.P. Rousseau of the 1st Canadian Parachute Battalion, whose fate, after being separated from his unit on the night drop, has never become known.

In recognition of the sacrifice made by these 359 men, their widows and mothers received the Canadian Memorial Cross.

The Broken West Wall.
Painting by Capt O. Fisher. Copyright THE CANADIAN WAR MUSEUM/12416

---

2   Bruce Tascona and Eric Wells, *Little Black Devils* (Winnipeg: Fry Publishing, 1983), p.146.

Abbreviations

AWARDS

CBE	-	Commander of the Order of the British Empire
OBE	-	Officer of the Order of the British Empire
MBE	-	Member of the Order of the British Empire
DSO	-	Distinguished Service Order
DSC	-	Distinguished Service Cross
MC	-	Military Cross
DFC	-	Distinguished Flying Cross
DCM	-	Distinguished Conduct Medal
MM	-	Military Medal
BEM	-	British Empire Medal
MID	-	Mention in Despatches
LH	-	Legion of Honour
C de G	-	Croix de Guerre

UNITS

Chaud	-	Le Régiment de la Chaudière
CHO	-	Cameron Highlanders of Ottawa (MG)
NSR	-	North Shore (New Brunswick) Regiment
QOR	-	Queen's Own Rifles of Canada
RCAF	-	Royal Canadian Air Force
RCN	-	Royal Canadian Navy
Regina	-	The Regina Rifles
RWR	-	The Royal Winnipeg Rifles
Tps Coy	-	Troops Company RCASC
1 C Scot	-	1 Battalion, The Canadian Scottish Regiment
1 Para	-	1st Canadian Parachute Battalion
5 F Coy	-	5th Canadian Field Company RCE
6 CAR	-	6th Canadian Armoured Regiment
7 CIB	-	7th Canadian Infantry Brigade
8 CIB	-	8th Canadian Infantry Brigade
10 CAR	-	10th Canadian Armoured Regiment

12 FA	-	12th Canadian Field Artillery Regiment RCA
13 FA	-	13th Canadian Field Artillery Regiment RCA
14 FA	-	14th Canadian Field Artillery Regiment RCA
14 F Amb	-	14th Canadian Field Ambulance
16 F Coy	-	16th Field Company RCE
18 F Coy	-	18th Field Company RCE
19 FA	-	19th Canadian Field Artillery Regiment RCA
22 F Amb	-	22nd Canadian Field Ambulance

GENERAL

A/Sergeant	-	Acting Sergeant
A/Cmdr	-	Acting Commander
CSM	-	Company Sergeant Major
F/L	-	Flight Lieutenant
F/O	-	Flying Officer
H/Captain	-	Honourary Captain
LCA	-	Landing Craft Assault
LCI	-	Landing Craft Infantry
LCT	-	Landing Craft Tank
L/Corporal	-	Lance Corporal
L/Sergeant	-	Lance Sergeant
Lt-Col	-	Lieutenant Colonel
Lt-Cmdr	-	Lieutenant Commander
Maj-Gen	-	Major General
P/O	-	Pilot Officer
RCA	-	Royal Canadian Artillery
RCAMC	-	Royal Canadian Army Medical Corps
RCASC	-	Royal Canadian Army Service Corps
RCE	-	Royal Canadian Engineers
S/L	-	Squadron Leader
WO	-	Warrant Officer.

Index of Awards

Surname	First Name	Rank	Award	Unit	Page
Adair	Robert William	Private	MM	NSR	28
Amos	William Alfred	L/Corporal	MM	18 F Coy	54
Aris	James Edwin	Sergeant	MM	Tps Coy	70
Armstrong	Walter Douglas	L/Sergeant	MM	Regina	44
Balmer	David Henry	WO	DFC	RCAF	13
Bartolacci	Harold Joseph	L/Corporal	MM	16 F Coy	34
Beverley	Henry John	Corporal	MM	6 CAR	51
Bishop	Craig	Lieutenant	DSC	RCN	85
Blackader	Kenneth Gault	Brigadier	DSO	8 CIB	76
Blake	Vincent James	F/L	DFC	RCAF	13
Blakely	Harold W.	Private	MM	NSR	26
Bond	Tom	Captain	MC	19 FA	60
Bray	William Roy	Major	DSO	10 CAR	27
Brooks	William Dudley	Major	DSO	6 CAR	52
Buell	Donald Bowie	Lt-Col	DSO	NSR	76
Burk	Charles Arthur	Lieutenant	2nd Bar	RCN	85
Butland	Charles Herbert	Private	MM	NSR	62
Chaffey	Donald	Lieutenant	MID	RCN	85
Chaplin	Harold Roe	Gunner	MM	19 FA	40
Chapman	Garbutt	Corporal	MM	6 Fd Coy	46
Chicoski	William	Riflemen	MM	QOR	39
Christian	Alexander S.	Captain	MC	10 CAR	63
Clark	George Stanley	Private	MM	NSR	64
Clarke	Lewis Gordon	Lt-Col	OBE	19 FA	78
Coveyduck	Walter Richard	Sapper	DCM	5 F Coy	34
Cowan	Leonard Elliot	Captain	MC	22 F Amb	41
Dalton	Charles Osborne	Major	DSO	QOR	38
Dalton	Hume Elliot	Major	DSO	QOR	37
Daughney	Ralph Herman	Major	DSO	NSR	61
Davie	J.C.	Lieutenant	DSC	RCN	23
Ducker	William	Private	MM	1 Para	15
Duval	John	Sapper	MM	16 F Coy	39

Fawcett	George Malcolm	Lieutenant	MC	NSR	62
Fitzpatrick	Hugh Morris	L/Sergeant	MM	5 F Coy	35
Forbes	Robert Borden	Major	MC	NSR	25
Foster	Harry W.	Brigadier	DSO	7 CIB	75
Foster	Raymond Donald	Sapper	MM	16 F Coy	68
Fulton	Lockhart Ross	Major	DSO	RWR	49
Godfrey	V.S.	Captain	MID	RCN	79
Goldie	Alexander G.	Major	DSO	12 F A	53
Gower	Philip Edward	Captain	MC	RWR	48
Grayson	William David	Lieutenant	MC	Regina	45
Hair	William Patrick	Captain	C de G	12 FA	52
Hanson	John Philip	Captain	MC	1 Para	15
Heaslip	John Leonard	Lieutenant	MC	22 F Amb	30
Herbert	William Grant	Lieutenant	MC	QOR	38
Hickey	Raymond Myles	H/Captain	MC	NSR	32
Holtzman	Jack	Gunner	MM	13 FA	45
Howes	Seymour Wylde	CSM	MM	16 F Coy	32
Jamieson	Graham Moffat	H/Captain	MC	Regina	46
Johnson	Oscar Albert	Riflemen	MM	Regina	43
Keller	Rodney F.L.	Maj-Gen	CBE	3 Div	74
Keller	Rodney F.L.	Maj-Gen	LH	3 Div	74
Killah	Alexander F.	L/Sergeant	MM	5 F Coy	34
Law	Charles Anthony	Lt-Cmdr	DSC	RCN	85
MacDonald	Douglas Bertram	Corporal	MM	22 F Amb	30
Macelwain	James Robert	F/L	DFC	RCAF	17
Matheson	Foster Martin	Lt-Col	DSO	Regina	76
Matthews	William H. V.	Captain	MC	C Scot	67
May	Lewis Farnell	F/O	DFC	RCAF	16
McClellan	Maxwell W.	F/L	OBE	RCAF	81
McTavish	Frank Alexander	Major	DSO	5 F Coy	33
Middleton	Robert Sherlock	F/O	DFC	RCAF	12
Mitchell	John	Lieutenant	MC	RWR	49
Moisan	Walter	Lieutenant	MC	Chaud	59
Moorehead	Charles H.	Riflemen	MM	Regina	44
Morton	Ronald Edward	Lt-Col	DSO	10 CAR	78

Mowatt	Charles F.	Corporal	MM	14 F Amb	57
Mutton	Jack B.	P/O	DFC	RCAF	12
Nickel	William H.	S/L	DFC	RCAF	12
Patterson	John Aubry	Captain	MC	NSR	29
Powell	John Wilson	Captain	MC	6 CAR	51
Proctor	Henry Archibald	Major	DSO	3 Div HQ	54
Romain	James Albert	Sergeant	MM	18 F Coy	54
Roseblade	Norman Leslie	F/L	DFC	RCAF	12
Runolfson	Helgi Stephen	Trooper	MM	6 CAR	52
Savage	Frederick S.	Corporal	MM	NSR	25
Schjelderup	Vilhelm Roger	Lieutenant	MC	1 C Scot	58
Seaborn	Robert Louden	H/Captain	C de G	1 C Scot	68
Semple	Alexander	L/Sergeant	MM	18 F Coy	53
Semple	Errol Quarrier	F/L	OBE	RCAF	79
Sevigny	Joseph Georges	Major	DSO	Chaud	66
Smith	Charles William	A/Sergeant	MM	QOR	37
Spencer	Ralph Charles	Sapper	MM	6 Fd Coy	44
Spragge	John Godfrey	Lt-Col	DSO	QOR	77
Storrs	Anthony H.G.	A/Cmdr.	Bar DSC	RCN	20
Synder	John Alexander	Sergeant	C de G	Regina	43
Tessier	Rene	L/Corporal	MM	QOR	39
Vennes	Bruno	Corporal	MM	Chaud	60
Walterson	Harley	Sergeant	MM	10 CAR	28
White	Franklyn E.	Lt-Col	DSO	6 CAR	78
Whittaker	James Edward	Lieutenant	MC	5 F Coy	23
Wonnacott	Gordon	F/L	DFC	RCAF	17
Woodward	James Crawford	Lieutenant	MC	CHO	66
Young	McGregor	Major	DSO	14 FA	40

Index of Formations

Air Forces

No. 414 Squadron, RCAF   16
No. 190 Squadron   12
No. 83 Group   16

Royal Canadian Army Medical Corps

22nd Canadian Field Ambulance   30
14th Canadian Field Ambulance   57
22nd Canadian Field Amublance   41

Royal Canadian Engineers, Corps of

5th Field Company RCE   3, 23, 33, 34, 35
6th Field Company RCE   44, 46, 50, 51
16th Field Company RCE   32, 34, 39, 68
18th Field Company RCE   53, 54

Royal Canadian Navy

29th Canadian Motor Torpedo Boat Flotilla   4, 83, 85
31th Canadian Minesweeping Flotilla   4, 19
528th Canadian LCA Flotilla   4, 23
529th Canadian LCA Flotilla   23
HMCS Prince David   4, 23
HMCS Prince Henry   4, 23, 79

Units, Armoured

1st Hussars (6th Canadian Armoured Regiment)   3, 6, 50, 51, 52, 78
Fort Garry Horse (10th Armoured Regiment)   3, 6, 27, 28, 63, 78

Units, Artillery

12th Field Regiment   6, 52, 53
13th Field Regiment   6, 45
14th Field Regiment   6
19th Field Regiment   6, 40, 60, 78

Units, Infantry

1st Canadian Parachute Battalion   3, 13, 15
Cameron Highlanders of Ottawa (MG), The   1, 66
Canadian Scottish Regiment, The 1st Battalion   1, 6, 57, 58, 67, 68
North Shore (New Brunswick) Regiment, The   1, 6, 25, 26, 28, 29
32, 61,62, 64, 76
Queen's Own Rifles of Canada, The   1, 6, 36, 37, 38 39, 77
Régiment de la Chaudière, Le   1, 59,60, 66
Regina Rifle Regiment, The   1, 6, 43, 44, 45, 46, 76
Royal Winnipeg Rifles, The   1, 6, 20, 47, 49

APPENDIX A

THE AWARDS [1]

A. ORDERS AND DECORATIONS

During the Second World War, the Dominion of Canada, as part of the British Empire, followed the traditions for awards available to officers and men of His Majesty's fighting forces. The tradition for awarding medals for gallantry began in the nineteenth century and gradually grew into an extensive system of military awards for recognizing gallantry in action.

The precedence of orders and decorations is regulated by the British Central Chancery of the Orders of Knighthood. Those awards mentioned in this book are defined as follows:

(1) Orders:

> Commander of the Order of the British Empire
> Officer of the Order of the British Empire
> Member of the Order of the British Empire
> Distinguished Service Order

(2) Decorations:

> Distinguished Service Cross
> Military Cross
> Distinguished Flying Cross
> Distinguished Conduct Medal
> Military Medal
> British Empire Medal

---

[1]   Source: Captain H. Taprell Dorling, *Ribbons and Medals*. (London: George Philip & Son Ltd.)

Order of the British Empire

The Most Excellent Order of the British Empire was founded by King George V, in June 1917, for services to the Empire at home, in India and in the Dominions and Colonies, other than those rendered by the Navy and Army. It could, however, be conferred upon officers of the fighting services for services of a non-combatant character.

In December 1918, His Majesty created a Military Division of the Order, specifically for all commissioned and warrant officers, for services which do not qualify for services in the field or before the enemy. Five classes were created which, for men, were designated as follows, with the right of using the appropriate letters after their names:

    (1) Knights Grand Cross (GBE)

    (2) Knights Commander (KBE)

    (3) Commanders (CBE)   for Major Generals, Brigadiers, and Colonels;

    (4) Officers (OBE)   for Lieutenant-Colonels and Majors, although higher and lower ranks may also be considered;

    (5) Members (MBE)   Majors, Captains, Subalterns, Warrant Officers.

Distinguished Service Order

This medal was established in 1886 for rewarding individual instances of meritorious or distinguished service in war by commissioned officers. Persons nominated had to be marked by the special mention of his name in despatches for "distinguished service under fire, or under conditions equivalent to services in actual combat with the enemy." The recipient may use the letters DSO after his name and bars may be awarded for further acts.

The Distinguished Service Cross

This decoration was instituted in 1901, originally as the Conspicuous Service Cross, as a means of "recognizing meritorious or distinguished services before the enemy" by warrant officers, acting warrant officers or by subordinate officers of His Majesty's Fleet. No person could be nominated unless his name had been mentioned in despatches.

In October 1914, its name was changed to the Distinguished Service Cross and the award extended to all Naval and Marine officers below the relative rank of Lieutenant-Commander, "for meritorious or distinguished services which may not be sufficient to warrant the appointment of such officers to the Distinguished Service Order."

In 1939, it was announced that the King had been pleased to approve that Commanders and Lieutenant-Commanders of the Royal Navy and officers of equivalent rank should also be eligible for the award of the Distinguished Service Cross. The recipients may use the letters DSC after their name and bars may be awarded for further acts.

The Military Cross

This decoration was instituted in 1914. It is an Army decoration and no person is eligible to receive it unless he is a captain, a commissioned officer of lower grade, or a warrant officer in the Army. Recipients are entitled to use the letters MC after their names and bars may be awarded for further acts. The original warrant provided for the award of the MC "in recognition of distinguished and meritorious services in the time of war." An amendment in 1931 laid down that it should be awarded to officers not above the rank of major "for gallant and distinguished services in action."

Distinguished Flying Cross

This decoration was established in 1918 for officers and warrant officers of the Air Forces recommended for "an act or acts of valour, courage, or devotion to duty performed whilst flying in active operations against the enemy." The letters DFC are used after the recipients name and bars may be awarded for further acts.

Distinguished Conduct Medal

This decoration was instituted in 1845 for "meritorious service", to be awarded on the recommendation of the Commander-in-Chief only to sergeants. The DCM for non-commissioned officers and men was sanctioned in 1854 to replace the old "Meritorious Service Medal" for gallantry in action. Recipients may use the letters DCM after their name and bars may be awarded for further acts.

The Military Medal

This medal was instituted in 1916 for award to non-commissioned officers and men of the Army for individual or associated acts of bravery brought to notice by the recommendation of a Commander-in-Chief in the field.

British Empire Medal

This medal was instituted originally in 1917, with a Military Division created in 1918. After several changes in form, in 1940 it was replaced by the current *Medal of the Order of the British Empire for Meritorious Service*. This medal was to be awarded in both a Civilian and a Military Division to persons who rendered meritorious service warranting a mark of Royal appreciation who were not already members of any of the five classes of the Order of the British Empire, and were not eligible for appointment to that medal. This medal could be awarded for gallantry away from the fighting line. Recipients use the letters BEM after their names. All ranks below that of substantive Warrant Officer (e.g. a Staff Sergeant) are eligible.

Mention in Despatches

This is an emblem denoting brave conduct granted under the authority of the Commander-in-Chief. It is represented in the form of a bronze oak leaf to be worn on the ribbon of the War Medal, 1939-45. No citation was required for those recommended for this award.

B. SPECIAL AWARDS

Lègion d'honneur

This award was established by Napoleon I, in May 1802, for rewarding distinguished military and civil services. The order is divided into five grades: "Grands Croix", "Grands Officiers", "Commandeurs", "Officiers" and "Chevaliers". The Legion of Honour is the premier order of the French Republic and is only conferred for gallantry in action or for twenty years' distinguished service in peace. The Order can be bestowed on foreigners. When given in war for services, it carries with it the automatic award of the Croix de Guerre with palm.

Croix de Guerre

This decoration was established by the French government in 1915 to commemorate individual mentions in despatches of French soldiers or sailors of all ranks, officers included, and also to officers and men of Allied fores mentioned in French despatches.

C. THE CANADIAN MEMORIAL CROSS

This Cross was established in 1914 "to be worn by mothers and wives of those soldiers who have died for the country's cause". It was presented to both the mother and widow of the soldier, sailor or airman who had been killed in action.

The central design is a Greek cross containing the royal cypher in the centre, with a crown surmounting the top arm and maple leafs at the ends of the other arms of the cross. A laurel wreath connects the arms as the background figure. It is a distinctive Canadian medal.

D. IMMEDIATE VERSUS PERIODIC AWARDS

Immediate Awards

The powers to confer awards of the DSO, MC, DCM and MM was delegated by His Majesty to certain General Officers for particular acts in a military operation. The Commander-in-Chief was to notify the War Office which, directly upon receipt of this notification, prepared a submission for the King's approval.

Periodic Awards

General Officers could accompany their Despatches with a list of recommendations for awards for services rendered during the period covered by the Despatch. Recommendations for Periodic Awards covered recommendations for gallantry in the field which, for various reasons, had not been conferred as Immediate Awards or in saving life other than in actual fighting with the enemy.

Bibliography

Barnard, Lt-Col W.T. *The Queen's Own Rifles of Canada 1860-1960.* Don Mills: The Ontario Publishing Co Ltd, 1960.

Byers, A.R., ed. *The Canadians At War 1939/45.* Westmount: The Reader's Digest, 1986.

D'Este, Carlo. *Decision in Normandy.* London: William Collins and Sons Ltd, 1983.

Bird, Will. *North Shore (New Brunswick) Regiment.* Brunswick Press, 1963.

Conron, Col A. Brandon. *A History of the First Hussars Regiment 1856-1980.*

Copp, Terry and Robert Vogel. *Maple Leaf Route: Caen.* Alma, Ontario: Maple Leaf Route, 1983.

Keegan, John. *Six Armies in Normandy.* London: Jonathan Cape Ltd, 1982.

Law, C. Anthony. *White Plumes Astern: The Short, Daring Life of Canada's MTB Flotilla.* Halifax: Nimbus Publishing Ltd, 1989.

Lawrence, Hal. *Victory At Sea: Tales of His Majesty's Coastal Forces. Toronto:* McClelland & Stewart, 1989.

Luxton, Captain Eric. *1st Battalion the Regina Rifle Regiment 1939-1946.* The Regina Rifles Association, 1946.

Munro, Ross. *Gauntlet to Overlord.* Toronto: The Macmillan Company of Canada, 1945.

Nolan, Brian and Brian Jeffrey Street. *Champagne Navy: Canada's Small Boat Raiders of the Second World War.* Toronto: Random House of Canada, 1991.

Roy, Reginald. *1944 The Canadians in Normandy*. Toronto: Macmillan of Canada, 1984.

Roy, Reginald. *Ready for the Fray: The History of the Canadian Scottish Regiment (Princess Mary's) 1920-1955*. Vancouver: Evergreeen Press Ltd, 1958.

Schull, Joseph. *Far Distant Ships: An Official Account of Canadian Naval Operations in World War II*. Toronto: Stoddart Publishing Co. Ltd, 1950.

Simonds, Peter. *Maple Leaf Up Maple Leaf Down*. New York: Island Press Cooperative Inc. 1946

Stacey, Colonel C.P. *The Canadian Army 1939-1945*. Ottawa: The King's Printer, 1948.

Stacey, Colonel C.P. Six Years of War. Ottawa: The Queen's Printer, 1955.

Stacey, Colonel C.P. *The Victory Campaign*. Ottawa: The Queen's Printer, 1966.

Tascona, Bruce and Eric Wells. *Little Black Devils: A History of the Royal Winnipeg Rifles*. Winnipeg: Fry Publishing, 1983.

Author Not Known: *The Fort Garry Horse in the Second World War*. Holland, 1945.

Wilmot, Chester. *The Struggle for Europe*. London: Collins, 1952.

Willes, John A. *The History of the 1st Canadian Parachute Battalion*. Port Perry Printing, 1981.

To order more copies of

VALOUR ON JUNO BEACH:
D-Day—June 6, 1944

by T. Robert Fowler

Contact:
GENERAL STORE
PUBLISHING HOUSE

499 O'Brien Road, Box 415
Renfrew, Ontario Canada K7V 4A6
Telephone: 1-800-465-6072
Fax: (613) 432-7184
www.gsph.com

VISA and MASTERCARD accepted.